New Jack Jocks

New Jack
Jocks

Rebels, Race, and the
American Athlete

Larry Platt

 Temple University Press
Philadelphia

Temple University Press, Philadelphia 19122
Copyright © 2002 by Temple University
All rights reserved
Published 2002
Printed in the United States of America

Library of Congress Cataloging-in-Publication Data

Platt, Larry.
    New jack jocks : rebels, race, and the American athlete / Larry Platt.
        p.   cm.
    ISBN 1-56639-954-8 (cloth : alk. paper)
    1. Athletes – United States – Biography.   2. Sports – Social aspects –
United States.   3. United States – Race relations.   I. Title: Rebels, race,
and the American athlete.   II. Title.

GV697.A1 P55 2002
306.4′83′08996073 – dc21

                                                    2001059236

All pieces have been significantly revised for inclusion herein.

Versions of "Pat and Allen's Tough Love Adventure" (May 1999), "Even
the Ball is White" (April 1999), "The Graying of Dr. J" (May 1993), "The
Unloved" (July 1995), "Soul Members" (August 1997), and "In the Name
of the Father" (June 2001) first appeared in *Philadelphia Magazine.*

A version of "No Requiem Necessary" (November 1997) was first published
in *GQ Magazine.*

Versions of "The Round Mound Bids Farewell" (April 2000), "Portrait of an
Artist on the Court" (July 2000), and "Jelly Maker" (September 1999) first
appeared on Salon.com.

Versions of "The Business of Rebellion" (November 1999) and "Magic
Johnson Builds an Empire" (December 2000) were first published in the
New York Times Magazine.

A version of "Spree's World" (December 1999) first appeared in *Men's
Journal.*

For Dad and P. J.,
the only two men allowed
to touch my remote control

Contents

THREE   The Entrepreneurs

New Jack Jocks

Introduction

IN THE FILM *Annie Hall*, the character played by Woody Allen is bored at a New York cocktail party of haughty intellectuals. He jokes dismissively that the journals *Commentary* and *Dissent* have merged to form *Dysentery*, then sneaks off to a bedroom to watch a Knicks game on TV. When his disapproving wife comes in, she wonders why he is drawn to a "bunch of pituitary cases running around in their underwear."

"Because they understand the physical," he replies. "These intellectuals are proof that you can be brilliant and have absolutely no idea what's going on around you."

Time and again over the past decade, I have felt like Woody Allen in that room – and not just because I too wear glasses and tend toward hypochondria. No, I relate to the Allen character because I have spent much of the past decade writing about sports in America and have consistently been struck by how sequestered the subculture is from the rest of American life, as though our games exist in a vacuum, separate and apart from the culture at large. In fact, I contend – and the following pieces prove – that sports can be a lens through which to see the country more clearly, if only we look closely.

While we are a country obsessed by the drama of sports, too often it is presented to us as little more than the American male soap opera, complete with its cartoonish heroes and villains. The result is a narrative offered up by the intelligentsia that posits our sports addiction – now a multibillion-dollar industry – as a mere diversion from truly important cultural matters. After all, inside American newspaper newsrooms, the Sports Desk is commonly called the paper's "toy department." Similarly, brilliant thinkers such as the renowned linguist Noam Chomsky suggest that sports is a part of the "indoctrination system . . . a way of building up irrational attitudes of submission to authority." No doubt Chomsky was among those from whom Woody was seeking refuge in the Knicks.

Today, the cultural elite goes even further, inundating us with hand-wringing about how deleterious our games have become. In the pages of *The Nation,* the normally clear-headed Katha Pollitt writes that "sports pervert education, draining dollars from academic programs and fostering anti-intellectualism. . . . For both fans and players, sports are about creating a world from which women are absent." In his book *Beer and Circus: How Big-Time College Sports Is Crippling Undergraduate Education,* respected Indiana University professor Murray Sperber goes so far as to suggest that collegiate sports' million-dollar TV contracts, leading to footage of war-painted, often drunken students whooping it up in the stands, actually imperil the state of higher education.

As Woody implied, when the subject is sports, these otherwise seminal thinkers just don't get it. This book is my rebuttal to them, a defense of sports on progressive grounds. For it has been my experience that, when it comes to the hot-button sociopolitical issues of our time, the sports subculture has been and continues to be ahead of the culture at large. It's actually been the breeding ground for progressivism, a laboratory for egalitarianism. I know this because I've seen it and written about it. And I know this because I've lived it.

IT IS, QUITE literally, the first memory of my life. I think I was six years old when I first saw him, this so-called draft dodger who so ignited the passion of others. It was 1969 and I was watching *The Dick Cavett Show* with my dad, a patriotic cold war Democrat, and my brother, a sixteen-year-old who, in two years' time, would grow his hair long–let his "freak flag fly," as Crosby, Stills and Nash would sing that very year–and join the burgeoning counterculture. My father is a World War II Coast Guard veteran, though an ironic one who likes to joke that he protected the shores of Seattle, where he was stationed, from Japanese attack; but as the show began, even he grumbled, VFW-style, about Cavett's guest, this draft dodger. Who was he not to serve? Who was he to question America?

A half hour later, though, something had changed. The guest forcefully and poetically repeated the arguments he'd been making on college campuses across the nation; I don't recall specifically what he said, but no doubt it was the full litany I've since read about, statements like "I ain't got no quarrel with them Vietcong" and "I will die before I sell out my people for the white man's money." Suddenly, the Vietnam War was being posited for what it was: the sending off of poor black boys to kill and be killed by other dark-skinned boys, all at the behest of a privileged white elite. Slowly, softly, as though to himself, my father started muttering, "He's right, he's right," over and over again. There sat my brother and I, wide-eyed, witnessing Muhammad Ali alter our dad's worldview.

But it wasn't just Ali back then who was teaching the post–Ozzie and Harriet nuclear family a new thing or two about America and values. Sports was an integral part of the changes being wrought by the power of pop culture; in music, Marvin Gaye, Sly Stone, and Bob Dylan had moved well past the penning of Top 40 ditties and morphed into social commentators. The same transformation was afoot in sports. As in music, sports provided an avenue for a new and different segment of society to burst into our consciousness and share a sense of what life was like from their side. John Carlos and Tommie Smith's defiant Black Power salute at the 1968 Olympics broke through the myopia of sports, as did Bill Russell's rejection of the sportswriter-fueled demand to be a "role model" – a thinly veiled repeat of the "credit to his race" label the white media had once placed on heavyweight champ Joe Louis. Similar was Joe Namath's embrace of sexual hedonism, which carried with it an implicit refutation of football's militaristic machismo – only Broadway Joe would don a pair of pantyhose for a TV commercial.

Of course, at the time the mainstream media failed to see the larger cultural role these athletes played; after all, it was that bastion of supposed liberal values, the *New York Times,* that insisted on referring to Ali as "Cassius Clay" for years after he dropped what he referred to as his "slave name." Indeed, Ali's moral legacy wasn't celebrated by the media until the mid-nineties, when, not coincidentally, he had already lost the power of speech and thus the ability to offend. The minute he became "safe" to the same press that had bashed him, he became heroic.

But as a six-year-old, I saw that my dad knew heroism when he saw it, no matter what the editorials said. And I know now that Ali wasn't an exception – that the twentieth century was, and the new millennium will continue to be, replete with examples of groundbreaking social lessons culled from our fields of play.

Take the issue of race, for example. As Ken Burns's documentary *Baseball* amply illustrates, the civil rights movement didn't start with *Brown* v. *Board of Ed.*; it actually began seven years earlier, when Jackie Robinson broke the sport's color line. Fifty-odd years later, the sports industry – primarily boxing, baseball, football, and especially basketball – is the most integrated sector of society, with the possible exception of the armed services. In fact, it's achieved a level of color-blindness the rest of the culture still aspires to. Kids receive an unambiguous message from sports: if you have the talent and work your ass off, you can make it to the NBA. While the odds are overwhelmingly against such success, discrimination, by and large, is not standing in the way. "One of the things I've enjoyed most about sports is that it brings the races together," basketball star Charles Barkley once told me. "In the locker room, we're all the same. It's all about merit."

And the triumph of color-blindness in sports has not diluted its celebration of multiculturalism. Many in the academy, for example, make passionate arguments for the legitimacy of black English in the classroom. Yet they seem unaware that it's a settled issue in sports: the dialect is accepted, even celebrated. "I can speak both ways," says NBA bad boy Derrick Coleman, who makes $9 million a year. "I can be in business meetings and be comfortable. But I choose to talk like I talked when I was comin' up with my homeys, even when I'm on TV. Because I ain't gonna forget where I came from." In other words, the patterns of speech that predominantly white sportswriters "clean up" from Coleman and others for their next-day stories are actually purposeful *and* political.

Today, such "race men" have become our foremost symbols of capitalism. Is there, after all, a labor union in the United States stronger than baseball's? During the 1998 NBA lockout (misreported, over and over again, as a "strike"), the owners jeopardized the season in pursuit of givebacks that would protect them from their own bad business decisions. It fell to Michael Jordan to make the case for the free market: "The owners paid these athletes what they felt they were worth," he argued. Those who can't afford to satisfy the market they themselves created, he maintained, ought to make way for owners who can. At a time when labor unions have fallen into widespread disfavor, athletes like Jordan have achieved rarefied status; they are working-class capitalists, performing as laborers – we see them toil every night – at the same time that they demand equity, or in sports' parlance "revenue sharing," with the owners.

The case for progressivism in sports is harder to make when it comes to gender, but there are encouraging signs for those of us who, as fans, recoil every time a headline heralds that another athlete has committed a sexual transgression. There is, for instance, the upsurge in popularity for women's sports, as evidenced by the U.S. women's soccer team triumph, the WNBA, the historic success of women's tennis (thanks to the revolutionary Williams sisters), and a few recent appearances of female placekickers on collegiate football teams.

Still, feminist thinkers such as Pollitt point to the O. J. Simpson case – not to mention countless other incidents in the world of sports where the woman is "other" – and argue that sports fuels a machismo that can lead to misogyny. A valid concern, no doubt, but one that finds fault with a subculture for simply reflecting ills that already corrode the culture at large. Besides, while many women complain about how emotionally closed men are, the men who play sports exhibit more emotion and tactile displays of affection toward one another than do other men in general. The sweet pre-game kisses between Magic Johnson and Isiah Thomas when their respective teams met in the NBA Finals made for titillating TV but also served a point: the stereotype of the macho Neanderthal no longer applies to the modern-day athlete. If sports fans were as at ease relating to their mates as athletes are relating to one another, sports wouldn't be about, as Pollitt and others maintain, an "us-versus-them" gender dichotomy.

TODAY I AM thirty-eight, and after a lifetime as a passion-ate sports fan, I have not, as Chomsky would suggest, seques-tered myself from the real world by escaping into *Monday Night Football.* Instead, sports' daily narrative has helped me find my way in that real world, constantly provoking me to examine what I think and believe. Throughout my lifetime as an armchair athlete, the way I've looked at the world has been informed by a steady stream of cultural antiheroes who just happened to run and jump for a living while wearing numbers on the backs of their shirts. If Ali was one of my first memories, Namath was perhaps my second, this wobbly-kneed, long-haired member of the counterculture who could throw the tightest spiral yet known to man. Not coinciden-tally, he was my brother Paul's idol; I remember how Paul, at sixteen, would mimic Broadway Joe's stoop-shouldered walk, and how I would try to do the same. Now I know that Paul was reacting to Namath's revolutionary presence in the same way a previous generation of teens had reacted to James Dean; here was the embodiment of cool.

As I got older, sports continued to connect me to the world, even as a body of literature came to suggest that its commercialization was a harbinger of dire social consequences. In the last few years alone have appeared John Feinstein's *The Last Amateurs,* which celebrates the nonscholarship college basketball of nearly all-white schools such as Colgate and Lafayette as somehow embodying the true essence of sports, and Mike Lupica's rant *Mad as Hell: How Sports Got Away from the Fans – and How We Can Get It Back,* which, by implication, idealizes the pre–free agency days when "pro" athletes couldn't earn enough for a year-round salary and the owners profited from their extreme labors.

The latest example of the trend is the aforementioned *Beer and Circus: How Big-Time College Sports Is Crippling Undergraduate Education,* by Murray Sperber. Sperber, long hailed as the voice of opposition to then Indiana University coach Bob Knight, argues that universities use sports to keep their students happy and drunkenly distracted – the educational mission of the university be damned. He quotes one student who defines his college education as a "four-year party – one long tailgater – with an $18,000 cover charge."

Absent from Sperber's fulminations is any sense of the integral role that "big-time" college football and basketball play in the undergraduate experience. I know this firsthand. I spent many a drunken night at the Syracuse Carrier Dome in the early to mid-eighties, cheering on the Orangemen – along with a similarly enthused audience that was easily the most multicultural gathering on campus. In the stands, blacks and whites hugged and high-fived, just as on the court. Moreover, these games linked us to the surrounding community; the barriers between the privileged college students and "the townies" broke down, as evidenced on the call-in sports talk shows, where guys from factories argued with students over whether the coach ought to have called a time-out when he did.

Sperber would have had me experience none of this valuable education. He has helped form the Drake Group, a consortium of academics intent on returning to the low-key style of intercollegiate competition now practiced in the Ivy League and at Division III schools such as Emory University and Hamilton College in central New York State, where, instead of athletic scholarships, a system of need-based financial aid – as for any student – is in place. Thus, Sperber runs the risk of undermining advances he championed in *Onward to Victory*, his book about Notre Dame football, where he illustrates how, through football, blacks first began to integrate the academy. Now, by pandering to an academic mindset still blinded by "dumb jock" stereotypes, he's at the forefront of a nostalgia for the good old days – days that left out everyone but White Anglo-Saxon Protestants.

Indeed, sports links the American male one to another in ways we rarely give voice to. We bemoan our athletes' bad behavior – and there is often plenty to bemoan: kids born out of wedlock, drug busts, even murder in one recent highly publicized case. We turn their transgressions into our object lessons, fashioning cautionary tales (Mike Tyson, Darryl Strawberry) or redemption stories (Jennifer Capriati). The intimate relationship we have to these modern-day fables links us all. We saw a youthful Charles Barkley deal with the ugly and raw reality of having spit on a little girl, and then we saw him grow over the years into a spokesman for family values. We saw Darryl Strawberry rise and fall time and again, valiantly dusting himself off after each near-knockout blow from a sickness called drug addiction. Many shunned him; I found him heroic in his battle against what he's conceded holds him powerless. Regardless of where you come down on Strawberry, grant me this: We ask our athletes to succeed or fail in the most public of ways at the most tender of ages, and they reveal character throughout the process, both good and bad. That, in part, is why we tune in; we don't know for sure what we would have revealed about ourselves under similar scrutiny in our early twenties. (I'm afraid that if an arena full of fans crowded into my office to watch me write, they'd come away with many complaints about what kind of person I am.)

While sports has linked me to other races and classes, it has especially connected me to two men in particular: my father and brother. To this day, we still spend hours talking sports, but just as when we watched Ali on *Dick Cavett* over thirty years ago, we're really talking about so much more. When we bemoan players jumping from team to team, we're really talking about fidelity, and when we opine on Allen Iverson's gangsta-rap CD controversy, we're revealing more about us and our predispositions on race and class than any political vote ever could.

Five years ago, the three of us went to a Phillies game. The Phils' Jim Eisenreich hit a grand slam and we all rose to cheer, then Paul whipped out a cell phone and began frantically dialing before screaming into the phone, "Eisenreich hit a grand slam! Eisenreich hit a grand slam!"

It turns out that for the last twenty-odd years, Paul has called his best friend from college, Mark, at big moments from live sporting events. Once, Mark's wife answered the phone and looked at him quizzically. "It's someone screaming, 'The ball's lost in the ivy,'" she said.

"Oh," Mark replied, matter-of-factly. "Paul must be at Wrigley Field."

I was reminded of Paul and Mark after spending some time with Ed Rendell, former mayor of Philadelphia and one-time chairman of the Democratic National Committee. Today, Rendell is known as a sports fanatic; he's hosted a TV football show and calls sports talk shows while on official government business. But even when he first ran for public office, Rendell understood something about sports and the American male. He understood that, viewed dispassionately, these games are silly; as comedian Jerry Seinfeld has observed, the players aren't even from the cities they represent. "So you're rooting for a shirt," he says. "You're cheering for laundry." Rendell knows, however, that the facts of the games are secondary. He knows that we use sports as a proxy for so much more; that's what Paul and Mark have been doing for twenty-odd years, and that's what Paul, my dad, and I have been doing since we shared those visions of Ali and Namath on a black-and-white RCA years ago.

"I remember when I first got into politics, when I ran against the incumbent for D.A.," says Rendell. "No one knew who I was. I would go to one neighborhood tavern after another and just talk sports to a group of guys. And then let them know I was running for something. I won, I think, because I was a sports guy, because I got it, and I got it because sports was always the one thing my son Jesse and I share most easily. You know, there's no generation gap. One of my all-time great sports memories was watching Penn play Michigan. It was Jerome Allen's sophomore year, must have been 1992–93. Jesse was twelve, and I had about five of my friends over to watch the game. And I remember watching Jesse interact with my friends as they all talked about the game, and I remember saying to myself, 'He now knows enough about sports to interact with adults.' I remember watching him in that room and I can't tell you how proud I was."

What follows is a travelogue of my journey in sports, culled from a decade of magazine writing. Here is Magic Johnson, hiring black people in inner-city neighborhoods; here is La-trell Sprewell, defiantly positing himself as the embodiment of the American Dream; here is Mike Schmidt, plagued by the media's corrosive cult of celebrity, and here is aging pugilist Randall "Tex" Cobb, finding wisdom and God and peace on the receiving end of yet another blow to the nose. In these and countless other cases, I remain resolute that there is much to learn from those who seem only to do phys-ical things for our mindless entertainment.

FOR THE FIRST TIME in his life, my friend Zack's nine-year-old son, Zane, was passionate about something: sports. "Other kids are playing Nintendo, and he's *reading*," Zack said. Zane became voracious; he buried himself in a biogra-phy of Randy "Big Unit" Johnson before moving on to coach Bill Parcells's latest tome, practically without pause. And then it happened: His teacher forbade him from reading an-other sports book, presumably in the interest of "rounding out" his interests.

What follows is for Zane, whose passion for this intricate world I still know; and for Woody, alone in that room with his Knicks while the pompous circulate just outside the door. Here's hoping that both say to their de facto adversaries – Zane to his small-minded teacher, Woody to the stuffy intel-lects – "Shuddup. Siddown. Learn from the game."

ONE

The New Jack Jock

1

Spree's World

WHERE WAS Latrell Sprewell? Days, weeks, *months* had passed without a word from him. Throughout the summer, the messages from his team, from companies offering multimillion-dollar endorsements, from the David Letterman show had stacked up on his cell phone voice mail. None were returned. Now it was fall, time for training camp in South Carolina: still no word from Spree. The media, the front-office brass of his team, the Knicks, even his teammates began to freak. Where could he be?

Streaking across the Nevada flats, that's where, nestled comfortably in his custom black CLK 450 Benz. The car was a cocoon that Spree had fashioned – like so many of his cars – in his own image. The tinted windows, the exotic tires (at over $1,500 each), the spectral blue headlights, and the hard-angled tail fused to the back end gave the ride a jarring, in-your-face look, somewhere between a Batmobile and a UFO.

Just as the worry in the Big Apple and the Carolinas reached a fever pitch, a summer squall hit out West. Spree put up the top, slid Biggie Smalls into the car's Eclipse sound system, with its thundering, glow-in-the-dark trunk amps, and – heedless of the storm swirling around him – entered

15

his own private zone. For the next ten or twelve or eighteen hours – he lost track – Latrell Sprewell flew as if through a dream, Biggie cranked, open road before him, calming landscape whizzing past. He was unconcerned, unhurried, unfettered and – for once – at home in his own skin.

Four months earlier, Sprewell's electric run in 1999's NBA playoffs provided a captivating villain-to-hero narrative of redemption. Two months before that, in a national sneaker commercial, Sprewell had tried to refute his thuggish, coach-choking image by looking into the camera while having his hair braided and saying: "Some people say I'm America's nightmare. I say I'm the American Dream."

After the craziness of the season, when he seemed to symbolize something to just about everybody, he needed the whole summer just to decompress. And now Sprewell, who'd been driving cross-country since high school whenever he needed to blow off steam, was ready, relaxed – even if the folks back east weren't. But Spree didn't feel compelled to soothe anyone. His philosophy, such as it is, has always been this: You can worry, get nervous, stress. But in the end, "it seems like the time goes by anyway."

IN PERSON, Latrell Sprewell makes and holds eye contact through droopy lids that seem to foreshadow narcolepsy. We are sitting in a lounge of the White Plains hotel where he keeps a two-bedroom suite during the NBA season, and where he spends most nights playing Sony PlayStation and building state-of-the-art stereo systems. On the court, Sprewell may be frenetic, even hyper; but here, a few feet from the garage where his two Mercedes and two SUVs are housed (eight other cars are either on the West Coast or back in his native Milwaukee), he is soft-spoken, thoughtful, and seemingly drained of energy.

Yet he is just as elusive as on the court. By the time we hang out, I've been camping out in the hotel lobby for days, receiving his polite regrets after he blows off each agreed-upon meeting. There is no trace of irony when at last he sees me not far from where he's parked one of the Benzes and, with utter insouciance, says, "There you are. I was wondering where you were at."

"So, you must really hate doing this," I say, turning my tape recorder on.

"Oh, man, I hate having to explain myself," he says, his mouth curling into a half-smile. "Why can't my game just do the talking for me?"

Those close to Sprewell often observe that there are at least two of him. There's the one sitting across from me, the oddly detached Spree, the one in the cool Cartier (nonprescription) glasses, whose lack of vocal inflection contrasts with the fiery on-court warrior Knicks fans fell for during the Finals run. This quixotic Sprewell is able to speak with clarity and insight about the Sprewell he prefers to be: Sprewell the metaphor.

When he choked P. J. Carlesimo, his coach on the Golden State Warriors in late 1997, he instantly supplanted the likes of Mike Tyson and Dennis Rodman as sports' preeminent public enemy. Almost overnight, this three-time all-star who had shunned publicity and endorsements, who had just wanted to play ball and be left alone, became a symbol. To some, he represented the worst fears of white America, the latest and maybe best embodiment of what poet Amiri Baraka (then LeRoi Jones) wrote over thirty years ago of boxer

Sonny Liston: "[Liston is] the big black Negro in every white man's hallway, waiting to do him in, deal him under for all the hurts white men, through their arbitrary order, have been able to inflict on the world."

The rhetoric denouncing Sprewell was not subtly coded. "[Sprewell's] appearance has gone full gangster," wrote a San Francisco columnist, ". . . with his braids and wispy sideburns. He's a hard shadowy figure." He instantly stood for how totally skewed professional sports had become, Exhibit A in an indictment of a generation of jocks seen not only as too black but too pampered, too lawless, too greedy. Rush Limbaugh denounced him on the air, and none other than William Bennett portrayed him in the pages of *Commentary* as symbolic of a nation's moral decay.

But then something happened. Traded to the Knicks, the severity of his punishment in the Carlesimo incident reduced by an arbitrator (from a cancellation of his long-term contract to the loss of sixty-eight games and $6.4 million), Sprewell found himself embraced by his new fans – even before his team started winning, even as the sports pages perpetuated the conventional image of him as a thug.

He was still metaphor, but by then a symbol of the sports press's myopia and dwindling influence. The fans had seen the fire of his game, and they'd seen him interviewed – you could almost hear the surprised chorus commenting on how "articulate" he was – and they'd taken in this corn-rowed, trash-talking bad boy because, behind the hip-hop packaging, he embodied hard work and passion.

Rather than reject his metaphoric status, Sprewell launched a personal image counterattack in a national sneaker commercial for the upstart, rebellious company And 1. Positing himself as the embodiment of the American Dream while, in the background, piercing electric guitar notes mimicked Jimi Hendrix's rendition of the "Star Spangled Banner," Sprewell tried to respin his story from that of dark menace to misunderstood rebel.

Yet, in person, he seems to be neither. Unlike, say, Charles Barkley or Allen Iverson, Sprewell's rebellion is decidedly . . . *passive.* His game is in-your-face, sure; but off court he's laid back, even lethargic, as if his exertions on the court require extreme conservation-of-energy measures off it. Unlike many NBA stars, Sprewell doesn't travel with an entourage or "posse." Those few who know him well often speak of just how detached he is, how he seems to walk through life as if on ether.

Now, thinking back on the controversy surrounding his yearlong banishment from the NBA, Sprewell seems tired. "It was mind-boggling," he recalls, stroking the tail of the corn rows that dangle behind his neck. "It seemed like it came from everywhere, the way that snowball just got bigger and bigger and kept on rolling faster and faster down that hill."

Though he speaks of the judgments that rained down on him as his "vilification," he shows no emotion, as if it all happened to a character in a movie he's watching. When I wonder what it feels like suddenly to be seen in the popular mind as representative of all that has gone wrong in a culture, he just shrugs. "What can you do?" It's no doubt a shrug born of the fatigue that comes with living as a human, walking metaphor. And it also probably has something to do with his deep need to lose himself in the role we've assigned to him. You won't see Sprewell protest his portrayal or use our language to defend himself. Instead, you'll get shoulder shrugs and strange reminders that "the time seems to go by anyway" when he's a no-show. And it all makes sense, in a way. Detachment, after all, is the beaten kid's sanctuary.

LATRELL SPREWELL was six when his father, Latoska Fields, left their Milwaukee home, though he still recalls the beatings his father administered to him and his mother, Pamela Sprewell. "I don't want to make it sound like my dad was a total jerk and he beat my mom and us when he came home every day," Sprewell said in 1998. "But there were occasions that I remember abuse was going on that was too excessive."

Sprewell bounced around throughout adolescence. He lived with his mother in Milwaukee, where, he says, he again received beatings – this time at the hands of his mother's boyfriend. He went to Flint, Michigan, to stay with his father. But in 1986, Fields went to jail for possession of marijuana with intent to distribute. Sprewell lived with his grandparents in Flint before ultimately returning to Milwaukee, where he was a tall, circumspect, even enigmatic kid at Washington High, who didn't play basketball until his senior year, when he earned All-City honors. It led to a two-year stint at a Missouri junior college and then a scholarship to the University of Alabama.

"We weren't the poorest, but we weren't the richest either," Sprewell recalls of his youth. "Put it this way: I've seen poor families and people in hard times and I know what real hard times are. I've basically been on my own. It kind of prepared me for the NBA lifestyle of being on the road. It makes living in a hotel like this not a big deal."

On the eve of the 1999–2000 season, Sprewell inked a five-year, $61.9 million deal with the Knicks; the long-term security prompted a pledge to buy a house in White Plains by season's end. But even then he'll live a solitary, nomadic lifestyle, touching down for at least part of the off-season in the house he owns in a Milwaukee suburb. His mother lives there year-round with Sprewell's fiancée, Candace Cabbil, with whom he has three kids. Also living with them is Sprewell's second daughter; he fought for, and won, custody of her after her mother, Sprewell's junior-college girlfriend, had gone to jail. His first daughter, born while he was still in high school, lives nearby, and Sprewell remains close to both her and her mother.

But he's never in one place for too long. It's part of a self-protective streak that goes back to a childhood where he learned that moving targets rarely get hurt. Now that he's rich, he's especially guarded. "I've got a huge family and it's like a lot of them want to try and invade my immediate circle now because of my success," he says. "And I just think, 'Okay, you may be a distant cousin, but don't just come in and act like we're buddy-buddy now. I respect you as family, but I can't say I'll treat you the same as one of my cousins I grew up with.' You have to be on guard. It's sad and you learn a lot about people."

So Sprewell keeps his distance. Those who are abused as kids often adopt masks to shield them from the world – and from their own pain. In Sprewell's case, it's always been the mask of the ultra-cool nonconformist. "As long as he has a fast truck and a leather jacket, he's content," says NBA star Chris Webber, a close friend.

Growing up, Sprewell related to those who sought to stand out from the crowd. "I remember wanting to be Drew Pearson, the Dallas Cowboys' wide receiver," he recalls. "He definitely had the coolest end-zone dance. He'd point his fingers like they were guns and fire them. Even in high school, I always had to be different. I can remember when everybody bleached their jeans. I'd bleach mine differently and put little rips in them, so even though I was kind of following the trend, I'd do something to make my stuff stand out. It's probably why I was one of the first guys in the league to wear braids. Even now, I don't want my cars, or anything I have, to be like anybody else's."

Sprewell senses that his lone-wolf style helps explain his popular appeal. "A lot of people like that person who doesn't just go by society's rules, so to speak, who finds a way to get their job done and still be able to do the things they want to do, be an individual," he says. "Everybody would love to be able to do our jobs the way we want to do it and not care about how our bosses or anyone thought about it. I mean, if you could do that, you'd do that in a heartbeat, wouldn't you?"

As I realized in that hotel lobby, Sprewell is on Spree time, and those of us who lead regimented lives – when are we not on schedule? – don't know quite what to make of such present-tense living. Waiting for him, I was much like the Knicks when he was AWOL last fall: nervous and pissed. Yet as much as his indifference prompts resentment, it also stirs a kind of muted admiration. At the same time that you resent him for messing with your time, you wish you had the balls to be so carefree, to choke a jerk of a boss, to blow off a bullshit work requirement – and still get paid gobs of money to work your ass off. If "Be Like Mike" is the acceptable norm, there's a deep, dark part of us that wants to be like Spree, because we know that the American Dream is no longer solely about rags to riches. It's still about attainment, yes, but it's also about achievement born of a ballsy, anti-establishment style; Bill Gates, after all, is celebrated as much for his renegade mindset as for the fortune he's amassed.

Which gives us Sprewell, a nonconformist in a culture –
professional sports – still wedded to the military model. No
wonder he had problems with a drill sergeant–type coach.
No wonder, too, that he's had a stormy relationship with the
media. Both coach and media tend toward a paternalistic
tone, a condition that prompts in Sprewell a sulky "I don't
care" attitude that is, after all, one of the hallmark legacies
left to abused children: detachment as weapon, an instinctive response meant to infuriate a tormentor.

That was the subtext in 1994, when his pit bull attacked
his daughter, then four, severing her ear. Sprewell was stunningly casual, shrugging and saying, "Stuff happens," while
his daughter was hospitalized. In reality, he says, he was re-
sisting the call to make his grief a public commodity. His interlocutors had a script they wanted him to follow; like the
detached but defiant child he once was, he refused to cry
"Uncle" – even though he was feeling the very emotions they
were demanding of him. "My daughter didn't need cameras
at the hospital," he says. "But, really, I'm just blessed that
she's here. Every time I look at her, you know, I say to myself,
'It's a miracle.' But I don't feel like that's anybody's business."

In fact, a curious scene plays out in the locker room after
virtually every NBA game, one that carries the same scripted,
psychological dynamic as the dog scenario, but with the volume turned down: A sweaty, stressed-out pack of mostly
middle-aged white guys surround a freshly showered, half-
clothed, usually black athlete and ask him questions along
the lines of "What were you thinking when you hit that shot?"
The question is, of course, unanswerable because, as Sprewell and countless other jocks attest, the shot was made precisely because the athlete had overcome the chattering dis-
tractions of his own mind. So the players parrot back clichés,

and both sides appear unaware they are characters in a classic culture-clash narrative. The members of the media are doubly alienated from the young men they present to us: They can't fathom the circumstances of, say, Sprewell's beginnings, nor can they relate to the sudden riches he basks in today.

Into this adversarial relationship has stepped a wary, wounded Sprewell, who long ago learned the self-protective benefits of shutdown mode. He bought into none of the media strategies for the modern-day jock. With the exception of the And 1 ad, he's passed on endorsements. And at Golden State, he'd regularly brush past the panting journalistic pack. Time and again, Sprewell says, media members assumed that how he treats them is who he is, instead of decoding his game for what it reveals about him. "Playing ball shows you a lot about a person," Sprewell says. "You see a player's true character come out. Some guys tend to give in and other guys buckle down and compete."

It was clear from his first night in a Knicks uniform that the fans inside Madison Square Garden liked what they saw in Sprewell, a player with a sense of urgency, one who embraces big moments on the court. Where they saw work ethic, the pundits saw showboating. Sprewell likes to adopt American Dream language and call himself a "self-made player," and it's true. The summer before his senior year at Alabama, he made himself into a perimeter shooter by, every day, taking nearly five hundred shots from twelve feet. Then he'd take five hundred shots from thirteen feet, then fourteen feet – and so on, moving a foot at a time until his midrange game was deadly and his three-point shooting respectable.

Maybe the fans sensed that what they were seeing on the Garden floor wasn't a game with "neither purpose nor symmetry . . . an avant-garde jazz riff, played at high speed and with little discernible logic," as Sprewell's harshest critic, Mike Wise of the *New York Times,* called it, but only *seeming* purposelessness – just as the best jazz musicians actually practice prior to improvising in public. When I ask what he thought of Wise's article (which the reporter later apologized for in print), Sprewell again goes someplace else. He matter-of-factly says, "Didn't read it," while looking off in the distance through those protective, hooded eyelids.

"THERE'S NO closure," Sprewell said before his return to the scene of his infamy. It was the first time he was back in the Bay Area, facing his old team and coach – Carlesimo. True to form, Sprewell's matter-of-fact yet incendiary rhetoric flew in the face of conventional wisdom, which would have had him shake Carlesimo's hand, let bygones be bygones. Instead, when Carlesimo made himself available for such a scene, Sprewell retreated into himself once again, pretending to focus his attention elsewhere.

He knows that he and Carlesimo will forever be linked, and that – ever the metaphor – he and his ex-coach will long symbolize the passing of an outdated coaching style. Carlesimo comes out of a coaching tradition that is in danger of confusing discipline for control, and Sprewell is at the forefront of a generation of players who, raised on rap, see any type of disrespect as an assault on their manhood and a stifling of their creativity. A showdown was inevitable.

After the attack, Sprewell was hoping the controversy would spark a national discussion about the way some coaches treat players. "A coach has to understand who you can push, who you can't push, and who you can push a little," Sprewell says today. "You have to be a people person, because you have so many personalities to deal with. And I think that the coaches who are aggressive about the way they handle people, a lot of players in the NBA are not going to tolerate that. Because we're men, you know?"

According to the riveting, 106-page report of the arbitrator, the tension between Carlesimo and Sprewell had been building for at least a month. Carlesimo denies calling Sprewell "a fucking idiot," but there is testimony about Carlesimo's in-your-face coaching style, complete with a stream of expletives. When I press Sprewell for specifics about Carlesimo's tirades against him, he demurs, but his language recalls the pain of his youth. "It was more of an abusive relationship type deal, that I allowed myself to get into. The point of what he was saying is not really as important as the frequency of it. But once I'm at the point that I've been disrespected, I will say, once that switch has been flipped, I'm really hard to handle," he says, pausing, his eyes narrowing to slits. "I go into a whole different mode. It's, uh, it's nothing nice. I'm not going to sit here and say that, if I'm really pissed off and in a dogfight, you know, I'm not gonna scratch."

Our time together is coming to a close. Noting that Sprewell has twice sued the NBA, claiming that the harshness of its punishment was racially motivated (the suit has been thrown out of court both times), I suggest that maybe it runs deeper than race. After all, if you're more comfortable being seen as metaphor, people will make of you what they will. Some will see you as a threat, others as the American Dream.

Sprewell seems to like this idea, that he's a blank slate on which others can impress meaning. He smiles as he leads me to the garage, where he shows me the cool tires on his Benz, and where he amicably chats about how he likes to do a lot of his shopping nowadays over the Internet, so he never has to leave his room save for practice and the games.

The smile stays in place as he talks about himself as metaphor for one last time – subject and commentator, first and third person, all rolled together into one complex, vexing package. "I hear what you're saying," he says. "You know, Biggie has these killer lyrics that say he's really a gangster, but he's saying it so smooth and so easygoing that there's a flow you get wrapped up in. But what he's saying is totally violent, you know?"

Latrell Sprewell is still smiling while fixing me with a hard stare. "With me, I'm kinda the same way," he says, extending his hand and shaking mine firmly. "I carry myself in a laid-back way. But at the same time, you know there's potential for danger."

2

Soul Members

THREE MEN are sitting in the Men's Grille Room at the prestigious Aronimink Golf Club in Newtown Square, Pennsylvania, in 1997, and they are making history. They don't seem to be talking about much. Over coffee, they compare notes on the state of their games – "I worked with the pro on my slice, and I think I overcorrected," one says – and mouth familiar clichés: "Golf really is a good walk spoiled," another jokes.

But then the conversation turns to youthful memories. "I grew up a sunshine kid in Florida, in the projects across from Jack Russell Stadium," says Jimmy Macon, his right leg bouncing excitedly under the table. "We'd sneak into the stadium and grind a hole into the outfield dirt with a seven iron, and that would be our golf course. We were mad at them because they wouldn't let us in the bleachers. I remember when the Dodgers would come to town and we'd cut holes in the fence to see Jackie Robinson play."

"I can tell you my own Jackie Robinson story," says Ken Hill. "The Mills were one of the only families with a TV on Spring Avenue in Ardmore, where I grew up. It was a Dumont with a slot for quarters in the back. So all of us from the neighborhood would collect our quarters and go over to the Millses and load that TV up on quarters, because you needed enough to watch a three-hour ballgame. That living room would be just jammed with people, because Jackie was about to play ball."

This room, this club, have been here for 101 years, and the walls, no doubt, have heard many golfers recall their youths. The air may even have filled with such reverential talk of Jackie Robinson, though those conversations were likely carried out *sotto voce* by the black caddies or waiters employed here.

But those doing the talking now are heading for the links. Macon, Hill, and Earle Bradford are about to play golf here, at one of the nation's most elite – and historically exclusive – clubs. They are making history because they are three black men sitting together, where no other three black men have before them.

A CROWD HAS gathered on the veranda overlooking the first tee. Onlookers dressed in Izod shirts and pressed pants sip iced tea while eyeing the unusual sight before them. The golfers can sense they have an audience.

"You never get totally used to it," says Macon, one of two black members at Blue Heron Pines Country Club, just outside Atlantic City. "I played [Haddonfield, New Jersey's] Tavistock four times, and you feel a little uncomfortable there. The guys get a little funny about you using their locker. Just this morning, when I was pulling into the parking lot here, three women saw me and did one of these"—he whips his head around twice in an exaggerated double take that prompts laughter from his partners—"and that is always going to be there. Tiger Woods ain't gonna change that."

Ken Hill, the sole black member at Aronimink and the first black admitted, back in 1991, to a formerly exclusive local club, pulls a driver from his bag and glances at those watching him. "I've been here six years now, and there's still a little novelty, I guess," he says, taking a practice swing. "I don't find it particularly uncomfortable, but it can get distracting when you just want to retreat to your club for some relaxation."

It is silent when they tee off. As the golfers walk the fairway, the curious crowd recedes; out of view, they become three guys on the links, but they are never just that, not really, and they know it. They are the first wave of blacks to integrate the most exclusive of golf country clubs. Like Ed Polite at Radnor Valley, or Jerry Johnson at Stonewall, or Ken Bacon at Philadelphia Cricket, or even the mysterious black member at Merion (the club did not return phone calls), these men are, depending on your point of view and on the effect they ultimately have, either pioneers or tokens. Even they are not sure which.

"It's a good question," mutters Bradford, fifty-one, the only black member at Philadelphia Country Club.

"I would say, if we were tokens, they wouldn't be charging us," says fifty-six-year-old Macon, and the others laugh and shake their heads in agreement.

"The fact is, we just don't know yet," says Hill, fifty-nine. "The one bone of contention I have is that I don't know if there's much of an effort made to sponsor or look for other

African American members. I heard there was one here in the pipeline who opted not to go through the process. So my guess is, we'll know about our legacy fifty years from now."

SIX YEARS ago, the story was the stubborn refusal of elite area golf clubs to change with the times. Despite the rise of the black middle class in the twenty years prior to 1990, most clubs seemed to be in accord with the view of Hall Thompson, founder of Alabama's Shoal Creek Country Club. In a 1991 interview, Thompson pledged that his club would not be pressured into admitting blacks, saying, "That's just not done in Birmingham, Alabama."

Thompson had given voice to the de facto policy of every big-time club in the country. Professional golf's governing bodies—the USGA, the PGA, the PGA of America, and the LPGA—tried to stem the tide of bad publicity by requiring clubs that were interested in hosting their lucrative tournaments to adopt anti-discrimination policies. They were up against long-held traditions, however. Three months after Thompson's comments, Aronimink withdrew as host of the 1993 PGA Championship, one of the sport's four major tournaments, saying it could not comply with the new minority-membership requirements for at least seven years, the anticipated length of its waiting list. Four months later, Merion Golf Club withdrew as host of the 1994 Women's Open because it would not promise to have minority members by then.

Recently, race and golf coalesced again in the national consciousness when Tiger Woods burst onto the tour with a $43 million Nike endorsement deal and the ubiquitous "Hello, World" commercial, in which he says, "There are still golf courses in the United States that I am not allowed to play because of the color of my skin."

Though the ad is not entirely true (if you're Tiger Woods, you can play anywhere, including the exclusive club in Newport Beach, California, where he is an honorary member), the fact is that, in the years since Shoal Creek, the story has ceased to be about such overt exclusion. Instead, across the country, clubs such as Aronimink and Merion have learned to do just enough to comply with the sport's governing bylaws – admit a token member or two.

"It doesn't surprise me that the Philadelphia region has so many clubs with just one black member, because with Merion and Aronimink, you're really talking about one of the nation's most elite areas for golf," says Marcia Chambers, a columnist for *Golf Digest* and the country's most preeminent chronicler of discrimination among the country-club set. (Her book *The Unplayable Lie: The Untold Story of Women and Discrimination in American Golf* paints a damning portrait of the second-class membership afforded females at many of the same clubs that admit blacks on a token basis today.) "The trend now is to have one black member so you can qualify for tour events. That's what happened at Aronimink and Merion. The key is going to be what happens when that first black tries to sponsor other blacks."

So far, progress on that front has been minimal. At St. Andrews in Hastings-on-Hudson, New York, Darwin Davis, a black executive at Equitable Life Insurance, has sponsored five blacks, all of whom were granted membership. But St. Andrews is the exception. In part, it's still too early; for instance, given the convoluted rules of their clubs, Hill and Bradford aren't yet full members. Radnor's Polite tried to sponsor two prospective black members, but one moved away and the other never formally applied.

There is also a limited number of blacks interested in joining these former bastions of exclusive privilege. "I'm the only black member at my club, and they've told me to go out and find members of color, and I haven't been able to," says John Merchant, the first black to sit on the executive board of the USGA and now one of Tiger Woods's lawyers. Merchant belongs to Fairfield Country Club in Connecticut, after spending fourteen years at another exclusive club that he declines to name. There, he sponsored three blacks for membership; all were denied. Merchant resigned after a mole on the membership committee told him they were turned down because of race.

"There are not a lot of black folk I know who can afford this," he says. "I'm on the hook to find one so I can avoid the tokenism issue, and I can't. But the clubs bear some responsibility, too. Most of them would take a black member, but they aren't out there actively seeking them."

It's not just the cost that's a barrier to minority membership. At Aronimink, for example, the roughly $25,000 up-front fee and $3,500 in yearly dues eliminate a lot of wannabes, but so does the arcane interview process. To be considered, you have to be sponsored by a member, seconded by another, and in possession of five letters of recommendation from others. That's a lot of networking, especially for members of a racial group that's been locked out of power for so long.

"It is not inexpensive to join these clubs," agrees Bradford, an executive with Arco Chemical whose own experience illustrates that even when money and networking are not the issue, time-worn racial issues still predominate. Five years ago, he belonged to Commonwealth Country Club in Horsham, where a number of blacks, including former 76ers coach Fred Carter, play. One of his underlings at Arco belonged to the more prestigious (and, for Bradford, convenient) all-white Philadelphia Country Club. He asked if the club was ready for a black member; the answer came back as no. He kept inquiring, however, until the answer was a lukewarm yes. With the support of a handful of members, including a retired Arco executive, he was admitted.

Now, on the third tee at Aronimink, Bradford's ears perk up when he hears Macon explain why his experience at Blue Heron Pines has been rewarding. "When I first went there, it sort of was uncomfortable," says Macon, who built up a successful plumbing, heating, and fire-protection business before retiring four years ago to play golf every day. "But now I feel like I'm the most special, special person there, 'cause everybody loves me, and I love them. It's really something that I wish a lot of my brothers could feel. See, it isn't phony when people actually get to know you."

"You know, I hadn't thought of it like that," says Bradford. "Golf is a common interest, and it makes it easier to talk to each other, blacks to whites, and vice versa."

Golf as a salve for racial wounds? It's not as far-fetched as it may sound. Time and again throughout this century, the subculture of sports has prodded the culture at large into social progress. In some cases, sports have even fueled social change. Think Jackie Robinson, the Black Power movement at the 1968 Olympics, or Billie Jean King's dismantling of Bobby Riggs.

As much of a pioneer as Tiger Woods may be, there are countless trailblazers at golf clubs throughout the country: men like Bradford, Polite, Johnson, Bacon, Macon, and, most of all, Ken Hill, vice president for community relations at Sun

Oil, who entered Aronimink in 1991, right on the heels of Shoal Creek. "I was used to being the first black to do a whole host of things," he says from the rough on the fourth hole. "The biggest challenge for me was trying to master this damn game. As you can tell, it hasn't happened yet."

I FEEL LIKE Anita Hill. I am sitting across from Aronimink president John Trickett, who looks eerily like Senator Orrin Hatch, only without the warmth. We are in the club's ornate Great Room, sipping sodas. Like Hatch, Trickett tends to leap into filibusters about "our country," about how good people like Ken Hill are for "our country" – when, that is, he is not reminding me that what I really want to do is "take a positive look" at the issue of country-club membership.

On the phone prior to our meeting, Trickett made the case that his club does not discriminate. "We'll let anybody in, but we have a process that we follow, and that includes a waiting list," he explained. "Why, you probably don't want to include this in your article, but we even have an Indian at the club who is a wonderful, wonderful doctor. I haven't actually met him, but I understand he's a wonderful doctor and a great guy."

Now, sitting with him on the admittedly breathtaking grounds of his club, I realize – his first impression perhaps notwithstanding – this is not a story with a bad guy. We talk about Tiger; we shake our heads over Mike Schmidt's obsession with the game; we share sympathy for Greg Norman, who will never live down what is arguably the biggest choke in the history of sports – his collapse at the 1996 Masters. John Trickett is an affable guy who, at sixty-six, is adjusting to a new world.

He grew up in Havertown, went to Haverford High School, and went on to own a lumber company. This club has been his life. His daughter, Anne, works here; he points her out as the "pregnant girl in the pro shop." (He mentions that Anne may name her baby after her mother, who died when she was twelve. "I had to be both mother and father," he says, "something I'm afraid I wasn't really cut out for.") He is a Main Line blue blood through and through. This diversity stuff feels new to him, but he's trying it on just the same.

"It's tough to find them," he says about black golfers. "Maybe fifty years from now there will be a lot more African Americans entering clubs, but it's difficult. Any change is difficult. People just didn't grow up that way. It's a difficult time we're all going through, but I think it's great, too, because it's good for our country."

We talk some more about golf's allure, something I've never quite gotten. On my way out, he mentions his one complaint with Ken Hill. "Ken's a heckuva guy, and I just wish we would see him more," he says. "I think he's a little reticent, being the only black member. And I can understand that. It's a hard thing."

Dwight Eisenhower was president when Ken Hill first thought about what might be happening on the grounds of Merion Golf Club. Hill had grown up on Ardmore's Spring Avenue, in the shadow of the prestigious club, but he might as well have been across the country; no one ever spoke of the fancy cars gliding by the South Ardmore playground, with their sets of golf clubs perched in the back seats. In fact, it was his neighbors' noticeable refusal even to acknowledge the presence of the club just up the road that conveyed the message to Hill: We're not wanted there.

South Ardmore in the years just after World War II was the closest the Main Line has ever come to a mini–melting pot. It was a predominantly black, Italian, and Irish neighborhood; generally, the blacks were the chauffeurs, the Italians the gardeners, and the Irish the maids at the ritzy estates that made up the Main Line.

Hill's mother was a maid and his father, John Hill, was a chauffeur, when he wasn't going from odd job to odd job; he'd work at the military-vehicle assembly plant on Lancaster Avenue, on the current site of the Ardmore shopping center, or as a cook at the Main Line Seafood House. In his spare time he bred dogs. Meanwhile, his son observed his work ethic, and when a young Ken Hill would ride his bike past Merion Golf Club or the tony estates in Bryn Mawr and Radnor, he'd stop and gaze at the mysterious grounds before him and think, I don't know how, but someday, I'm going to get me a piece of this.

Though discrimination was widespread, it wasn't really palpable to the kids from Spring Avenue. Sure, they noticed that they'd be called to play in the Lower Merion High football games for the second and third quarters, after the starters – the white boys – began getting their asses kicked. In the fourth quarter, the starters would reenter the game, their uniforms still pristine, and bask in the applause for a win they hadn't really earned. And they noticed when one of their neighbors, a successful black pharmacist, was not allowed to buy a house in the new development in Havertown.

But what awaited Hill and his friends outside the relative calm of the neighborhood would open their eyes. In fact, growing up with whites – "living in multiple worlds," Hill calls it – served him well when, after graduating from Temple University, he was hired by Sun Oil and assigned to call on service stations in Royersford, where news of the gains being made in the Jim Crow South seemed like a well-guarded secret. In some cases, station owners would take a look at the new Sunoco salesman – a 6'7" black man – and ask where he played basketball.

"Oh, I was the captain of my chess team in college," Hill would deadpan.

Other times he would simply be told: "I'm not doing business with niggers."

"Well, then you won't be getting your shipment of gasoline," Hill would reply calmly.

"My size meant they could only go so far in trying to offend me," he recalls today. "And thanks to where I grew up and the lessons I learned, I knew they were just trying to provoke me to the point of failure. If I had whipped off my tie and said, 'Let's go to war,' they would have won."

Eventually, Hill became Sun Oil's first black district manager, and later its first black division manager. When he was transferred to Michigan in 1975, one of the perks of the promotion was membership in an exclusive golf country club; by that time, Hill had already learned the value of golf in cultivating business relationships. But because of his skin color, he couldn't have the golf membership. Instead, he was offered a membership at an area tennis club, which he accepted. Other blacks – certainly those of future generations – might have balked. But Hill kept his eyes on the prize.

"I liked tennis at the time," he says. "And I was really just concentrating on my career, on what I could do to move ahead."

So, while colleagues equal in all matters save skin pigmentation were reserving tee times, Hill was relegated to taking clients to the tennis courts. "I've always been a pragmatist," he says. "And coming of age in corporate America, you learn to get places by being polite and following rules."

In 1980 he was transferred back to Philadelphia, and three years later he was named Sun's first black vice president. Throughout the eighties, he played golf often but never really thought about joining a club, until, in the aftermath of Shoal Creek, Sun chief executive officer Robert Campbell asked him to join Aronimink.

"If I'm going to remain a member there," Campbell told him, "they're going to have to open their doors. If I'm going to sponsor other executives, they're going to have to let you in."

Hill mulled it over. He remembered the time he was playing at another area club as a guest and a member approached him, saying, "My shoes are over by my locker."

"I'll do yours if you do mine," he had responded, before walking away.

He knew that, given his career trajectory, he should have been asked to join a country club years before. Should I defiantly refuse? he wondered to black friends, few of whom could understand why (to mutate the Groucho Marx line) he would join a club that wouldn't have any of them as a member.

Finally, his wife, Irene, asked, "What's the worst thing that can happen?" He realized that at an upper-crust, patrician club such as Aronimink, painful racial confrontations would be unlikely. He thought, Those opposed to letting in a black will probably just ignore me; hell, I've been dealing with that my whole life – that's on *them*, and who better than me to pioneer in this way, someone who has always been the lone black face in the boardroom?

Ken Hill took his CEO's offer of sponsorship, saying, "Somebody has to be first."

EARLIER, WHEN the three black golfers were in the Grille Room, two of them nodded in understanding assent when Ken Hill mentioned that his father would be doing cartwheels if he could see his son today, a member at one of the very clubs John Hill used to make deliveries to – around back.

But now the same group of men has returned to that room, and they're not talking about their race or their backgrounds. They are talking about golf, and their laughter can be heard in the adjacent locker room and pro shop. They are, simply, golfers. One, Jimmy Macon, is explaining why he doesn't play in a regular foursome every day.

"My first year, I was playing with a group of guys, and I had to tell them I already had a family, you understand?" he says. "The same guys would be eating lunch off me every day. That's tiring."

"Right, right – I already fed my kids, huh?" says Earle Bradford.

"See, I'm particular about who I play with," says Ken Hill. "But part of that has to do with the fact that I don't have much confidence in my game."

Macon smiles. "Let me tell you something," he says. "I played with this eighty-year-old guy a couple of weeks ago. You know how, when you're not playing too good, you tend to start apologizing? Well, this old-timer says to me, 'Jimmy,' he says, 'I been playing this game for sixty-odd years, and ain't nobody give a shit's shit about what you shoot – they're too busy worrying 'bout they own damn score!'"

Bellows of laughter carry through the clubhouse. To those hearing it, including John Trickett's daughter in the pro shop, it is a familiar sound, the sound of golfers happily playing hooky from the office or escaping the routine of home. The men doing the laughing, however, know otherwise; they are here telling stories and rehashing every shot on every hole, as countless generations of golfers have before them in this very room, and they know there is no mistaking the sound of their laughter. It is the sound of change happening.

3

Pat and Allen's Tough Love Adventure

LET'S START with what they've chosen to burn into their skin. After all, few people nowadays consciously live their lives in accordance with a firm moral code; fewer still advertise that code on their bodies. But the young black millionaire, jailed at seventeen for a crime he didn't commit and brought up in unimaginable poverty, and the middle-aged white millionaire, reared in a shot-and-beer world where raising hell in local taprooms was considered proper etiquette – these two do live by code: It's right there on their arms.

On the middle-aged white millionaire's left forearm is a colorful pirate ship. "It means no rules," he says, his eyes wide and bulging with the intensity of his ethic. "It means getting the job done. No matter what way. It means being a warrior."

On the young black millionaire's left forearm is a panic-stricken skull, frozen in mid-shout, with a red line across it over the words "Fear No One." "That's me," says the young black millionaire, whose raspy tough-guy voice masks a passion rivaling the older man's. "That's why it's got the red line through it. 'Cause you'll never catch me like that, fearin' anything."

The older man says he sees a vulnerable kid beneath the young man's macho pose – a pose he knows firsthand. The young man says the older man is not just another suit: He's led a life.

They may look like an improbable couple, the sullen-seeming thug from the 'hood and the overexuberant rich guy from the whitest part of town, but Allen Iverson and Pat Croce have more in common than the gulfs of race and generation that should divide them. "We're soul mates," says the older man. And it is a story, this partnership, that just might transform Philadelphia in a way that transcends sports.

THERE MAY have been a time, long ago, when our sports teams played a game and won or lost, and then everybody moved on. No longer. Now we obsess on sports all day, every day, and it's not the game that matters as much as the underlying narrative. We're addicted to the stories on our fields of play, to tales of noble failure, pampered excess, heartwarming redemption.

If Pat Croce, president of the Philadelphia 76ers until his resignation in the summer of 2001, knows anything, it's that people want good stories. He's constantly reminding us of his own, about a kid from the wrong side of the opulent Main Line tracks who went from the training room, where he was taping ankles, to the boardroom, where he owns the team. And now comes Act 2, his unlikely alliance with a twenty-something superstar, a storyteller in his own right, a rapper whose self-expression has sparked a firestorm of controversy. Together, they've woven a tale that is long on drama, as they've resurrected a once-mighty sports franchise and challenged the psyche of a city.

Call it "Pat and Allen's Tough Love Adventure," an unscripted narrative that recalls Philadelphia politics circa 1991, when a flawed but charismatic cheerleader took over a moribund city and, through indefatigable effort and positivism, reinvigorated it. Like Ed Rendell, Croce and Iverson inherited a disaster and set about fixing it with an un-Philly-like absence of cynicism. And like Rendell's story, this one has been played out before the cameras, with ever-increasing stakes. But that's part of the story, too: Both Croce, who had the audacity to believe he could buy a professional sports team, and Iverson, who has the guts to challenge much bigger and nastier players under the boards, live for the gamble.

Their narrative begins in 1996, when Croce and Iverson, in Croce's words, "were rookies together." Croce was popular, but Iverson was sports' latest poster boy for misbehavior. He had burst onto the court as the basketball embodiment of gangsta rap, a corn-rowed hip-hopper who insisted on hanging with his homeys even as their run-ins with the law gave him bad press.

While his signature move – the blindingly quick "crossover" dribble – thrilled fans, it was anything but revealing of his larger societal role. He was, in fact, a walking reminder that the days of *cultural* crossover, when black stars such as Julius Erving and Michael Jordan sought and won white acceptance, were over. Iverson was leading a new generation of ballplayers, kids much less interested in acquiescing to white, mainstream taste, kids who scoff upon hearing that Erving shaved his Afro in the late seventies when he decided he wanted to be a businessman. It is a constant theme in rap music: Selling out and forgetting where you come from is anathema. So you won't see Iverson losing the corn rows because they turn off businesspeople, any more than Croce toned down his wild-man persona to appease boardroom tastes.

Yet Croce says that Iverson, baggage and all, can bring Philadelphians together across racial lines in a way no one has since Erving. (Barkley, who insisted on speaking out about race, divided the city during his reign.) For Erving, that 1983 championship parade down Broad Street was the glorious culmination of his crossover dream. And now Croce, Erving's former personal trainer, has caught crossover fever. Croce will drive into North Philly, he says, not far from where he was born, into neighborhoods where some white suburbanites might be frightened of the waves of black people running after his car and pounding on the hood. But he loves it, because he knows what they want: high fives and tickets, which he almost always carries with him for such purposes. And he knows the excitement is largely because of Iverson.

"When he does one of his spectacular moves, I love to look around the stands and see whites and blacks hugging each other and high-fiving," Croce says. Philadelphians appreciate work ethic, Croce maintains, and Iverson is nonstop hustle on the court. And it doesn't hurt that he comes with the imprimatur of Croce, a working-class Philly hero.

Croce believes that the backlash against Iverson is actually part of a much bigger picture. People forget that generational handoffs are a natural phenomenon. In fact, in the mid-seventies, legendary Celtic coach Red Auerbach "dissed" the gold-chained, Afro-ed Erving for his "playground style," seeing it as incompatible with winning.

Well, Erving went on to make that playground style a fundamental part of the game, and Jordan built on his innovation, on and off the court. It is easily forgotten that in 1985, Jordan showed up for his first all-star game not in an Armani suit and Kenneth Cole shoes but in baggy jeans and a backwards baseball cap. Croce knows that, similarly, Iverson is of his time. It makes sense, after all, that the demeanor and game of today's best player would reflect the in-your-face aggressiveness of the music he was raised on.

"I won't tell Allen Iverson how to express himself," Croce said, a lone voice of reason after news broke of Iverson's hard-core rap CD. There Iverson stood on the opening day of his team's 2000–2001 training camp, cornered by a bewildered press pack about the rhymes he had written, refusing to discuss his CD, saying that, with the exception of the rap-specific press, no one in the media "understands hip-hop because they don't want to understand hip-hop."

The scene amply illustrated the respective combatants in a cultural and generational chasm. On one side are Iverson's overwhelmingly white and middle-class interlocutors, who have reacted (without hearing his CD in full context) to his rhymes literally and ahistorically. On the other side of the divide are a generation of young black artists who have created an art form – hip-hop – with cultural mores all its own.

Iverson has been denounced – one columnist called him a "thug with money" – for the following words, which appeared in *Sports Illustrated* magazine: "Never mistake me for a fake MC / You got the wrong identity / Nigga, I'm CT / Get murdered in the second and first degree / Come to me with faggot tendencies / You be sleeping where the maggots be. . . . Now I'm reaching for heat / Leave you leakin' in the street / Nigga screamin' he was a good boy / Ever since he was born / But fuck it, he gone / Life must go on / Niggas don't live that long."

The NAACP, gay and lesbian groups, and veteran civil rights leader C. Dolores Tucker, who has partnered with self-appointed morality czar William Bennett in a war against rap, organized a protest. Iverson issued an apology, saying he never intended to offend anyone and that he doesn't advocate anti-social behavior, and agreed to meet with the groups. He did – though Tucker was a no-show.

From Iverson's flummoxed perspective, all this hand-wringing about hip-hop's content misunderstands the art form. Chuck D, pioneer rapper of the group Public Enemy, once said that hip-hop was the "CNN of the ghetto"; it uses literary technique to tell gritty, sometimes offensive stories that are, above all else, a real depiction of inner-city street life. That's what Iverson is doing, as evidenced by his CD's original title, *Non-Fiction.* (In the aftermath of the controversy, Iverson has since announced he would not release the CD at all.)

Nearly 70 percent of rap records are bought by white kids in the suburbs, in large part because it's an authentic travelogue into another culture. Those consumers are aware of the multiple fictions used to tell these stories. They know, for instance, that Eminem is an artist who, as a matter of story-telling technique, has created the character of Slim Shady, a rap protagonist who often mouths offensive lyrics for dramatic effect, like countless characters in popular movies. Similarly, we get Iverson's alter ego, Jewels, presenting a snapshot of street life that has brought down this torrent of judgment on the basketball star.

To Iverson's way of thinking, he is an entertainer. The Answer is his basketball character; Jewels is his rap alter ego. (In fact, the CD's cover reads: "Allen Iverson *as* Jewels.") Could it be that the controversy over Jewels's rap is proof of a deep-seated cultural animus toward young black men who wear the hip-hop uniform? After all, the media mavens who have gone so apoplectic about Iverson were conspicuously silent when the Lakers' Rick Fox played a murderer on the violent HBO series *Oz*.

Through Jewels, Iverson chronicles a violent underworld, which is not necessarily the same thing as endorsing violence. Indeed, the character of Jewels is based on the Samuel Jackson character in the film *Pulp Fiction;* only, in Iverson's storyline, Jewels is a "lyrical hit man"–that is, he kills other MCs with the power of his rhymes. Ironically, in his compelling book *I Feel Great!* Croce tells some uproarious stories about his own violent youth. There are recountings of barroom brawls, not to mention the time police escorted Croce from the state of South Carolina after he'd decked a redneck who proceeded to fire a gun his way. There is, rightfully, no outrage over Croce's storytelling, in part because the context is understood: he's weaving a narrative, not advocating antisocial behavior. In reality, there's not much difference between Jewels's stories and Croce's: Both regale in graphic ways that, out of context, could offend.

They're both storytellers, the older white millionaire and the younger black one. At first glance, there is no ostensible reason why Croce should–unlike so many in the media–look beyond his generation's anti-rap rhetoric and see Iverson in full context. Croce, after all, may be one of the whitest guys in pro sports. He had one black friend in high school, and his "I feel great" rah-rah shtick has a decidedly Caucasian ring. His idol is Jimmy Buffet. But his life experiences allow him to see beyond the clichéd portrayal of Iverson as the NBA's embodiment of Thug Life. He sees, instead, a sweet, shy, and surprisingly responsible young man behind the corn rows, gold chains, and ultra-cool, loping walk, whose raps just happen to reflect the culture in which he was raised. And Pat Croce wants others to see Iverson that way, too.

WHEN HE RE-SIGNED with the 76ers for $71 million over six years in 1998, Allen Iverson didn't mention Larry Brown, the coach with whom he'd just begun to form an uneasy alliance. No – at a time when most superstars exhibit disdain for their teams' ownership, Iverson credited his. "Pat had a lot to do with my signing this contract here," the prodigy says now, dressed in typical hip-hop garb: baggy jeans, Timberlands, an Enyce sweatshirt. "From day one, he kept it real with me. He didn't shoot me no curves. He didn't come in and kiss my ass or try to show me that he wasn't gonna kiss my ass. He just ain't phony." Such comity seemed a distant dream a little over a year before, after Iverson blew off a practice in New York. Before the next game, Croce came to Boston and personally read his young superstar the riot act – but not without a typical flourish at the end. They were in the locker room, just the two of them, and the players on the other side of the door were a little amused, a little confused.

"Do you believe I care about you?" they heard Croce shout. Iverson mumbled an affirmative response, but not to Croce's liking. Philadelphians have long known about Croce's shouts; we've heard "I feel great" echoing off the rooftop of the First

Union Center and radio airwaves. Now Croce would wait, face to face, until Iverson said it as if he meant it.

"I need you to answer out loud!" Croce screamed. Back and forth they went, until Iverson shouted back.

"I needed his mind to hear him say it," Croce recalls, his voice echoing off the walls of his office as it must have in that locker room. "I grabbed him by both shoulders, crowding his space, staring into his eyes. Because he's got to know that I love him and if I'm mad, there's a reason. He didn't grow up *sitting around the dinner table, saying grace and 'Pass me the mashed potatoes'!*"

It was just a sample of the strategy Croce employed with Iverson, a careful mix of straight talk and soothing understanding, a tough love that takes into account and even plays to the star's belief that he's no more than a commodity to a whole bunch of people – most of them white guys in suits. ("I was the prey," Iverson told the *Inquirer* when he dismissed agent David Falk, the man who changed sports by fixing Michael Jordan up with Nike.)

In everything Croce does, it seems, he keeps Iverson in mind. Just before re-signing Iverson a couple of years ago, Derrick Coleman and his ho-hum attitude were jettisoned, despite Brown's affinity for Coleman's basketball smarts. Some connected with the team suspected the move had Croce's fingerprints. Coleman made it hard for Iverson to buy into Croce's rah-rah way of doing things, the thinking goes.

Now, after games, Iverson talks about defense and frequently takes responsibility for his own miscues. The old image of Iverson as selfish – none other than Croce's friend Barkley once dubbed him "Me, Myself, and Iverson" – has become passé. Iverson has even adopted Croce's sayings. "I'm going to play every game like it's my last," Iverson pledges over and over again, echoing a favorite Croce mantra. "If you imagine today is the last day of your life, you're going to take advantage of it," the owner often preaches.

Not that there haven't been issues. Once, after Iverson missed a practice, the player was deeply hurt by the ensuing media squall, the questions about just how much he'd matured. His girlfriend Tawanna Turner had had a miscarriage, and his bodyguard phoned in his excuse. Yet Brown and a couple of unnamed teammates blasted Iverson in the papers without talking to him first.

He scoured the news for Croce's comments. And just as he expected, he saw no public criticisms. "He kept it in the family," Iverson says. "I respect Coach Brown. He's my coach, and I've learned a lot from him. But for whatever reason, Pat just knows how to handle himself. If he's gonna rip me, he'll rip me man to man. And I'll sit there and take that. But he won't go to the paper and try to tear me down, because he already knows they're not for me, they're against me. That's okay. People been against me my whole life. So it would shock me for him to talk about me like that."

For his part, Croce saw the controversy as a way to advance the narrative. Both Brown and Iverson, he realized, could benefit from the fallout. To Iverson, he talked about responsibility – including calling in his absences himself, like the man he yearns to be treated as. "And Larry and I talk, and I say, Larry, why say that in public? We're a family," says Croce. "Allen should have been upset, and because he was, it became my issue to bring it up with Larry."

As a physical therapist, Croce became skilled at motivating and manipulating powerful people. His high-visibility role as trainer to Philly's stars was a dress rehearsal for dealing with Iverson. "I was successful as a physical therapist, not because I knew about ultrasound, but because I knew I could get into your head and make you feel better, which is the beginning of healing," he says, unable to sit still behind his desk. On the wall behind him is a giant photo of Jimmy Buffet onstage, wearing a Sixers jersey; under that is a photo of Croce and "Bubbachuck" – Iverson's childhood nickname – clowning around on one of Pat's Harleys. "Allen's not one you can tell something to, like, 'This is the way you've gotta do it,'" Croce explains. "He's more, 'Let me live the experience, good or bad, endure the pain, and I'll learn from it.' His rookie year was the yin. Now we're getting the yang."

It hasn't been all yang, however. At one point, Iverson, playing hurt, reportedly muttered, "About fuckin' time,"when Brown put him back into a game. Brown reacted defensively, seeing Iverson's aside as a threat to his authority. Within days, both men were publicly on the same page, but the incident didn't bode well for the future: Brown, the old-school coach, with a history of relentlessly riding and chiding his best players, was again unable to communicate effectively with his overly sensitive hip-hop superstar.

"You can't have a good marriage without communication," says Croce. So Croce concentrates on communicating with the player who is his future. Before games, Iverson and Croce huddle together in the training room, a ritual that means a lot to Iverson; he checks the clock, awaiting Croce's arrival. On this evening, Croce shows up and recounts an incident from a half hour ago, when "two big black guys" somehow found their way into his office. "One guy said they'd come to pick up VIP passes that [Sixers general manager] Billy King left for them," he explains. "So I picked up the phone to call Billy and the guy starts saying, 'Well, I don't really know Billy King.' I stood up and said, *'You're fuckin' lying to me! Get out of here!'* And these guys were big, Bubba. I just grabbed each one and *tossed them the fuck out!*"

Iverson is laughing so hard that he is doubled over. But beyond the shared laughter, the story reinforces a theme: the toughness that comes from always being the little guy. When he was Iverson's age, after all, black-belt Croce was renowned for kicking butts he could barely reach.

Usually absent from the daily Croce/Iverson confab is talk of basketball. Once in a while, Croce compliments the star on his assists or his defense – anything but his league-leading scoring, which everyone else praises him for. "I have no right to talk to him about his game," Croce says.

They could, however, discuss posse management. When I first broached the subject of this article to Croce, he broke into a wide smile and invited me to his suite in the First Union Center, where guys like Meat and T-Bone – longtime riding buddies in his weekend Harley-Davidson gang – were hanging with him. "They're *my* posse," Croce said. In the summer, they're all getting on their Harleys and trekking cross-country to California. "There's one state we've gotta go around, because one of the guys isn't allowed in," Croce explains a bit sheepishly.

The travails of Iverson's own posse have been widely chronicled. There was the arrest of Andre Steele and Michael Powell, who were allegedly using Iverson's Mercedes in a drug deal, for instance. These aren't seen as the kinds of friends who bring in the corporate endorsement contracts, but both men, says Iverson, were good to his family during his own time of trouble, when he was locked up for four months at age seventeen on a bogus charge stemming from a bowling-alley brawl in which witnesses said he wasn't even involved. Then-governor of Virginia Douglas Wilder commuted the five-year sentence, and Iverson's record was later expunged by the courts, but the effects of incarceration are still with him today. They're one reason for his guardedness, especially with strangers, which includes the media. "I'd be distrustful of white people, too, if one of my first experiences with them was them putting me in jail for something I didn't do," Croce notes.

So Iverson continues to trust those who knew him before the millions. It's a familiar inner-city story, really: The outlaws protect and nurture the neighborhood prodigy, making sure he doesn't blow his opportunity and end up like them. That's how it happened with former NBA great Isiah Thomas, who had some rough characters screening for him in the Chicago ghetto where he grew up. "Allen is like me – loyal to a fault," Croce says a bit proudly.

Still, Croce purposely introduced Iverson to a couple of his own buddies from long ago, guys he once had to cut loose until they pulled themselves together. "These guys wouldn't stop powdering their noses," Croce told Iverson. "I had to tell them I couldn't hang out with them anymore, that they were bringing me down and true friends wouldn't do that. Now we're friends again, because they got their lives together."

Try as he might to empathize, not even Croce can comprehend the circumstances of Iverson's upbringing in Hampton, Virginia. There, the famed crossover dribble had its tragic roots: The reason the kid was playing basketball day and night was to avoid going home, where there was no electricity or heat or plumbing – a home where raw sewage floated on the floor. Every day was perilous: One summer, eight of his friends were killed. His mother, Ann, was fifteen when she gave birth to Allen; his father, Allen Broughton, had little contact with his son before being sentenced in 1998 to nine years in jail for stabbing a former girlfriend. Michael Freeman, the man Iverson considered his daddy, the man who taught him basketball, went back to prison in 1999 for violating parole, having been convicted eight years before of drug possession with intent to distribute.

"I grew up on the tough side, *but not like that!*" shouts Croce, who hails from a working-class section of Lansdowne. "We had running water. My dad was there, and he'd beat me if I didn't do the right thing. I don't know how I'd have turned out if I didn't have a father at home—I'm a little rough around the edges anyway, and that was *with a dad!*" Croce wasn't much younger than Iverson when he was kicked out of the dorms at West Chester University for putting two bigger guys in the hospital. "I didn't have a clue when I was this kid's age," Croce says.

It is after another Sixers win, another stellar Iverson performance. Croce and his wife, Diane, stop by the family room, where the players' wives, girlfriends, and children wait. When five-year-old Tiaura Iverson sees Croce, she bursts into a wide smile: "Uncle Pat Croce!" she yells. But her attention is soon diverted when her father appears, not much more than a kid himself, dour expression firmly etched on his face. Tiaura runs to him, though, and the tough-guy pose melts, and Allen Iverson is laughing, cooing, and tickling his daughter as Croce looks on, providing commentary.

"How can this be a bad kid?" he says to Diane. "That smile is a reflection of what's on his heart."

Later, he will not be able to shake the image of this gangsta softy. *"You can't be a thug with that smile!"* Croce screams in typical understated fashion. *"I don't care how bad or cool you act!* He's like a watermelon – all hard on the outside, all soft and squishy and full of all that good red stuff – blood – on the inside, like a heart. This kid, he breaks you down, like that crossover dribble, when he smiles."

STIFF AND SULLEN, Allen Iverson has just finished practice at the St. Joseph's University field house. Now comes the part he least enjoys: answering the usual litany of questions from the press, a group Barkley refers to as "the flies" because they're always buzzing around.

"Y'all got any new questions for me today?" Iverson begins. They don't, and he delivers his one-word replies in a bored monotone. After the "flies" disperse, however, he comes to life: His eyes widen as if he's just seen a sliver of an opening in the lane, and his mouth expands into the grin that has so captivated Croce. I've asked about his kids.

"Deuce had a stomach flu," he says, explaining a recent, excused missed practice. Deuce is two-year-old Allen II; Iverson had stayed home to help Tawanna nurse him back to health. "Now, Tiaura, all she wants to do is go to Chuck E. Cheese all the damn time," he goes on. "There be a whole lotta noise in my house. All these kids do is run around and tear up the house. Man, Tiaura, I don't even have to say nothing to her, I just give her a look and she knows: 'I better calm my ass down.'"

The words come rushing out. This is the Allen Iverson who hasn't made it through the media filter, Croce and other friends maintain. Sure, we've read all about his on-court transformation, but those around him know there's been no epiphany.

Iverson, like any prodigy, is a work in progress. If he is newly mature, he explains, it has more to do with his kids than basketball. "They're everything to me," he says. "They've motivated me to grow up a lot faster. The experience I had in my life, all the shit I've seen, helped me grow up too, but I feel my kids put so much responsibility on me, 'cause I have to set a good example for those guys. So that makes me make better and smarter decisions."

Now that Iverson has divorced himself from agent Falk, the ultimate image maker, he has taken control of his own career. And he is the gravy train for a substantial extended family. In addition to Tawanna and their kids, Iverson provides for his mother and his two sisters, plus two uncles, not to mention an aunt and her three kids. They all live with him on the Main Line – as does the much-bemoaned "posse," the guys who have been in his corner since Hampton. And he'll provide for the man he considers his father when Michael Freeman gets out of jail.

Iverson is in danger of becoming Philadelphia's least likely exemplar of family values. What other hip-hop icon would put up with Ann, a peripatetic cheering section of one, wearing an Iverson jersey under the Sixers basket and holding a sign reading: "That's My Boy!"?

Then again, after Iverson's tumultuous rookie year, *some* change in image was inevitable. At the all-star game that season, he was booed mercilessly by fans who saw him as an arrogant upstart, devoid of respect for elders like Jordan. The reception devastated him. After the game, Sixers PR man Bill Bonsiewicz introduced Iverson to his mother, who was in town. That night Bonsiewicz sat on the team plane, frozen with trepidation, as Iverson made his way down the aisle, looking pissed. "Bill," Iverson whispered, taking the seat next to him, looking down. "You've got a great family. Don't ever take that for granted." He kept his voice low, Bonsiewicz thinks, because he was guarding that tough-guy image.

Children don't heckle or boo or judge, so it makes sense that Iverson is most at ease with them. He has started the Crossover Foundation in Hampton, a nonprofit that puts on charity events to keep the local Boys and Girls Club from closing. "I just want those little kids, who aren't fortunate enough to have resources other kids have, to know they have someplace safe to go, you know what I'm saying?" he explains and shrugs. "I don't do charity for the media, man," he says when pushed for more details. "I do it so the kids feel good."

What makes Iverson feel good? His spare time is spent drawing caricatures – a passion he says he'll concentrate on once his playing days are over. "I'm gonna focus on my art," he proclaims. And he's started a rap label designed to empower his friends. "These guys I grew up with, they got a lot of talent," says Iverson, whose car stereo has been playing a lot of popular rappers Redman and Jay-Z of late. "I didn't want them going out there in the music world and getting jerked around."

By the time we finish talking, we are alone in the gym. Outside, a pack of autograph seekers awaits. Iverson will wade through them, signing without breaking stride en route to his Bentley, and then it's straight home, where, if the kids are quiet, he'll get some solitude.

Later in the day, Croce will have a conversation with Ann, Allen's mom, just to make sure things are okay. Part of his job, as he sees it, is making sure she's happy.

"Is Allen high-maintenance? Yes," Pat Croce says. And then his eyes narrow to intense slits behind his appropriately rose-colored glasses, and he stage-whispers: "But most of the geniuses of the world have been high-maintenance."

TWO

The Anti-Hero

4

Portrait of an Artist
on the Court

ROUGHLY TEN POINTS is all it took for the Beast to rise. Until this moment, the Champions Senior Tennis Tournament in Central Park's Wollman Rink had been a sweet chance for tennis fans to revel in nostalgia. Here was Jimmy Connors at forty-seven, mock-limping to the delight of the capacity crowd of three thousand. There was the once-stoic Swede, Bjorn Borg, forty-four, actually laughing between points at Connors's antics. All grown up now, they parodied the solemnity of youthful rivalry. They had realized, finally, that it was only a game.

All except, that is, for the Beast. Friday night, June 16, 2000, should have been Johnny Mac night in New York City. The legendary John McEnroe had walked to the court from his Central Park apartment, Yankees cap pulled down tight. As so often happened throughout his playing days, he had been greeted by enthusiastic cheers from his hometown crowd. Yet a mere ten points into his match against Frenchman Henri LeConte, there was the graying, forty-one-year-old McEnroe, a doting father of six, doing something just as inevitable: Turning everyone against him by charging the net

– to question a lines call. "C'mon, Mac, not already!" a spectator called out.

McEnroe turned to the courtside fan, his face suddenly pale with rage. "You got an appointment to get to?" he said, spitting out the words through lips pursed in anger. "What the fuck do you care, asshole?"

The crowd erupted in boos and the umpire administered a code violation for unsportsman-like conduct, but it was too late: The Beast had been unleashed. For the next two hours, against all his intentions, McEnroe stalked the court, throwing his racket four times, berating a middle-aged linesman, and slamming a courtside sign advertising Sector Sport Watches ("Hey! Hit somebody else's sign!" someone yelled from the Sector Sport Watch company box seats) in dangerous proximity to a female tournament official, whom McEnroe then blistered with a series of choice condemnations of the "you fucking asshole" variety when she saw to it that he was penalized. He also, in between such dramatic acts, hit some of the purest and most creative shots a tennis court has ever seen and, once the match was over, refused to shake the umpire's hand, leaving a crowd that came expecting feel-good nostalgia but instead had been treated to the genuine, raw article.

Screw nostalgia, McEnroe seemed to say; just as in the eighties, when his combination of talent and temperament transcended his sport and he attained pop-culture icon status by turning tennis into performance art, McEnroe had again provided a voyeuristic glimpse into tortured genius.

It is no accident that, since leaving the tennis tour in 1992, McEnroe has devoted himself to rock music – writing and performing songs in New York clubs under the moniker the Johnny Smyth Band – and has opened a SoHo art gallery. He has always delighted in being called an artist; his authorized biographer, Richard Evans, once wrote that McEnroe is a "pointillist tennis player," referring to the school of art, fathered by George Seurat, in which the painter uses only the tip of his brush.

Similarly, McEnroe, who was renowned for rarely practicing or watching what he ate, dominated stronger, bigger, more committed players with a wholly instinctive game that was characterized by a feathery touch and a series of jabs and wrist flicks that produced unfathomable, sharply angled shots. "McEnroe saw the court in different geometric dimensions than anyone else," says Eric Riley, a former tour player who has coached Pam Shriver, Lisa Raymond, and the Jensen brothers. "On any given volley, the rest of us might choose between two or three shots. But somehow Mac would see all these possibilities that never occurred to anyone else before."

Yet, despite the seven Grand Slam tournament victories, the seventy-seven singles titles (third all time behind Connors and Ivan Lendl) and the No. 1 ranking from 1981 to 1984, it was the dark side of his artistry for which McEnroe became most widely known, the temperament that led him to be dubbed "McBrat" by the staid English press after he lambasted a stuffy Wimbledon umpire by screaming, "You are the pits of the world!"

It wasn't so much that McEnroe was supercompetitive; his rage for perfection in himself and others was just as likely to explode when he was winning. The tirades would invariably be followed by public soliloquies of introspection ("Why did I let it happen?" he wondered once, after the Beast had run amok), showing both an innate intelligence and a stunning tendency toward self-flagellation. Behind the blowups was a self-loathing narcissism ("I'm so disgusting, you shouldn't watch. Everybody leave!" he screamed between points during the 1981 Wimbledon tournament) and a class resentment in reaction to tennis's pretensions. He would rail against the sport's "phonies and elitists," earning him anti-hero status.

He hung with Jack Nicholson and Mick Jagger, both of whom offered similar advice after he'd been banned from the Davis Cup in 1985 and there were rumors of a yearlong suspension: Don't ever change. ("When you're 26, who are you gonna listen to, Jagger and Nicholson or some old farts in the United States Tennis Association?" McEnroe recalled in *Sports Illustrated* in 1996.) Nike signed him up (his total career earnings from tennis and endorsements are said to surpass $100 million, well beyond what any other tennis player ever made) and graced Sunset Boulevard with a James Dean–like mural of Johnny Mac on a city street, the collar of his leather jacket turned up. It was a fitting image, because long before Dennis Rodman or Latrell Sprewell, McEnroe was sports' preeminent rebel without a cause.

JOHN PATRICK MCENROE JR. was born on February 16, 1959, at the U.S. air-base hospital in Weisbaden, West Germany, where his father was stationed in the air force. When John was nine months old, the family returned to Queens, New York, living first in Flushing before settling in Douglaston. John Sr. was Depression-era born and first-generation Irish American, both of which may help explain his eldest son's later patriotism–McEnroe is the all-time leader in Davis Cup wins–and his class resentments. The senior McEnroe worked a day job while attending law school at night and eventually became a partner in the prestigious Park Avenue law firm of Paul, Weiss, Rifkind, Wharton and Garrison.

John Jr. commuted to the tony Trinity School on Manhattan's Upper West Side. There, with its tweed-jacketed, pipe-smoking headmaster, McEnroe got his first taste of the stodgy upper class he'd later wage war against at Wimbledon. Yet he was well behaved in high school, the odd subway turnstile jump while shouting, "UN delegate!" notwithstanding. He was a stellar student who may have loved soccer more than tennis. But he fell under the tutelage of the legendary tennis coach Harry Hopman at the Port Washington Academy on Long Island and played junior tennis throughout high school. While his talent was clear, his dedication wasn't. He wasn't a top-ranked junior and even garnered a reputation for giving close lines calls to his opponents.

In the summer of 1977, before heading west to play No. 1 singles for Stanford, McEnroe went to England to try to qualify for Wimbledon as an unseeded player. The pudgy, unknown eighteen-year-old stunned the sports world, making it all the way to the semifinals – the first qualifier ever to do so – before losing to Connors in straight sets. The next year, as a freshman, McEnroe was tennis's collegiate champion and was soon challenging Connors and Borg, who were dueling to be ranked the world's greatest player. Meantime, McEnroe's temper had exploded enough times – and in close enough proximity to the court's microphones – that he soon supplanted the roguish and sometimes crude Connors as Public Enemy No. 1.

Certain catchphrases became legendary, launched like verbal artillery at blank-faced umpires. There was "You cannot be serious!" or "Answer the question! The *question!*" –

the word emphasized with as much venom as words alone can contain. There was the time at the French Open when he screamed, "I hate this country!" and the time he told a tournament referee to "go fuck your mother." And there was the inevitable contrition afterward. "I know I've got a problem," he told his biographer Evans, author of 1990's *McEnroe: Taming the Talent*. "When I walk out there on the court, I become a maniac ... something comes over me, man."

Yet the talent and the temperament seemed to work hand in hand. In exploding, McEnroe would create a drama with himself at its epicenter, and by raising the stakes, he'd more often than not raise the level of his play, as suggested by his first wife, the actress Tatum O'Neal. "All those negative responses, like 'I'm going to win because the crowd hates me, people hate me; I've got to beat the crowd, beat the officials,'" she lamented to Evans. "He makes life so difficult for himself."

But he won. In 1979, he won his first Grand Slam event, taking the U.S. Open. Then came the greatest match in the history of tennis, 1980's five-set marathon loss to Borg in the Wimbledon final. The next year, McEnroe got revenge against Borg at Wimbledon and beat him again at the U.S. Open, toppling Borg from the world's number-one ranking and sending the mysterious, stoic Swede into an early retirement at all of twenty-six. The rivalry with Borg, though brief, remains epic, because the two men were such a study in contrasts. Borg was the emotionless, patient baseliner; McEnroe the loudmouthed, net-rushing New Yorker. Borg was the master of the passing shot; McEnroe the possessor of the quickest and softest hands at the net, the toughest to pass. When Borg left the scene, aficionados expected McEnroe to dominate, but McEnroe missed the rivalry too much and went into his own funk. It was Connors, instead, who won the 1982 Wimbledon and 1982 and 1983 U.S. Opens. But McEnroe wasn't done yet. Though he is best remembered for the wars with Borg, it is 1984 that should be McEnroe's lasting legacy.

In that year, McEnroe may have been the best player ever. He won eighty-two matches and lost just three, the highest winning percentage (.965) since the dawning of the Open era. His 6–1, 6–1, 6–2 dismantling of Connors in the Wimbledon final was arguably the most dominating display in modern tennis history: Seventy-eight percent of his slicing first serves went in, most of them unreturned by the game's greatest returner, while, astoundingly, McEnroe committed only two unforced errors in the entire match. The angled volleys were sharper, the drop shots deadlier, the serve more meticulously placed than ever before. And this wasn't just anybody he was carving up on center court; this was Connors, one of sports' all-time competitors, who couldn't get back in the match. If all the tantrums and vitriol had come from the frustration born of perfection's elusiveness, then for that one Sunday morning in England, there was finally no need to scream at anyone.

In keeping with McEnroe's nature to see every glass as half-empty, he remembers 1984 as the year not of his greatest triumph but of his greatest regret. Up two sets to none, and five points from taking the match against Lendl in the French Open, McEnroe overheard voices on a television headset that was left unattended on the side of the court. Picking it up, he screamed, "Shut up!" into it – no doubt popping the eardrum of the poor unsuspecting technician at the other end – thereby earning the enmity of the crowd. "I have this unique ability to turn the whole crowd around," McEnroe said afterward to *Sport* magazine. It was to be one of the few times McEnroe was unable to overcome the opposition of a hostile audience. Suffering from heat stroke, he lost in five sets.

After that year's U.S. Open, McEnroe would never win another Grand Slam or be ranked number one again. It was as if the near-perfection of 1984 hadn't fulfilled him. More often than not, he seemed disgusted on the court. Brad Gilbert, now Andre Agassi's coach, describes an uproarious 1986 McEnroe meltdown in his book *Winning Ugly: Mental Warfare in Tennis.* Gilbert was the mirror image of McEnroe, a player short on natural talent but long on workman-like desire. "Gilbert, you don't deserve to be on the same court with me!" McEnroe snarled at his opponent during a change-over when it became apparent he might lose to him. "You are the worst! The fucking worst!" After the loss, McEnroe announced he was going on what turned out to be a seven-month sabbatical, because "when I start losing to players like him, I've got to start reconsidering what I'm doing even playing this game."

By then, the game of tennis was changing. Pure power players such as Boris Becker, with his 125 mph serves, were ascendant, aided by new racket technology that increased power without sacrificing control. Though still one of the top two or three players in the world, McEnroe, with his artistic flair for finesse volleys and quirky angles, was suddenly a stylistic anomaly. In addition, for the first time in his life, tennis wasn't monopolizing all his intensity. In 1984, McEnroe met his temperamental equal in O'Neal, and the two wed in 1986 (the press dubbed them "Tantrum and McBrat") after he'd called her "the female John McEnroe." Indeed, she'd barred her father, the hot-tempered actor Ryan O'Neal, from the wedding when it was rumored that he'd called McEnroe "a jerk." After six years of marriage, five homes (including a Malibu beach house purchased from Johnny Carson for $1 million and three tennis lessons), and three children, O'Neal and McEnroe parted ways, ostensibly because she wanted to work and McEnroe wanted her home with the kids. "I've had a lot of experiences with men who are bullies," O'Neal told *Entertainment Weekly.* "Taking on John McEnroe was the biggest struggle of my life."

In 1992, while his marriage was crumbling, McEnroe reached the semifinals of the U.S. Open and led the United States to a rousing Davis Cup win over Switzerland. While other top American players, ranging from Connors to Pete Sampras, haven't always made the Davis Cup a priority, McEnroe led the Americans to five world titles in twelve years. Fittingly, the last great moment of his tennis career came during the 1992 Cup, when he played doubles with rising star Sampras. When the Americans won, McEnroe unfurled a giant American flag and ran laps around the court, waving it and screaming, the normally placid Sampras in lockstep.

Though he didn't officially retire, his tennis waned while McEnroe tried to find other outlets for his creative impulses. McEnroe had visited his first art museum in 1977, when his mixed-doubles partner and childhood friend, Mary Carillo, took him to a Claude Monet exhibit in Paris during the French Open. "I remember him standing in front of one of the great Monets and saying, 'You gotta be kidding, my brother Patrick has better stuff than this on the front of our refrigerator!'" Carillo told the *Guardian* in 1994. "But I guess he's coming around. He always did like to hang around eccentric, creative people."

Later, the late Vitas Gerulaitis, a fellow pro and New Yorker, started ushering McEnroe around SoHo galleries. He bought his first painting, by the realist Audrey Flack, at a gallery on Prince Street and began visiting museums and galleries nationwide while on the tennis circuit. In 1993, while separated from O'Neal, he apprenticed at a gallery on East 79th Street, spending all day looking at art. "I was really down and out at the time," McEnroe told the *Independent* in 1994. "I had just been separated and it was a Godsend to be able to go to a place and keep my mind off what was going on. Because of that, I became more interested in the idea of doing something on my own."

He opened the John McEnroe Gallery in SoHo the next year. "There are a couple of connections between art and tennis," McEnroe told the *Independent*. "People in the art business have a tendency to one day tell you you're the greatest artist that ever lived and the next second make you wonder if you'll ever sell a piece of art again. So I think I have a knowledge of that, because you have a fear when you go on the court: fear of failure . . . I understand [artists] are needy and insecure."

In recent years, McEnroe's passion for the business side of art has lessened. First, he shifted his focus to rock music; years ago, friends such as Eric Clapton had tutored him in guitar. He formed a band and began working on an album but inexplicably quit a couple of years ago. "I think it was a combination of fear of success and fear of failure," the band's manager told the *New York Times Magazine* early in 2000.

His foray into rock 'n' roll did introduce him to his current wife, Patty Smyth, who sang "The Warrior," a top hit in 1984. Together they have two children of their own, to go with McEnroe's three from his union with O'Neal and Smyth's daughter from her previous marriage. In 1996 the National Father's Day Committee, a New York nonprofit organization, named McEnroe father of the year. When he's not traveling these days, McEnroe can be found every morning walking his nine-year-old daughter, Emily, to school. "By having kids, I got my humanity back," he told *Sports Illustrated* in 1996. "I'd been like some tennis dude, No. 1 in the world and not happy with it."

Most recently, McEnroe has become reenergized about tennis, having been appointed Davis Cup captain, a position for which he's long lobbied. His first act was to convince the top two names in the men's game, Agassi and Sampras, that Davis Cup ought to mean something to them. When the U.S. team beat Zimbabwe in February 2000, there was McEnroe stalking the sidelines, earning a warning for bad language and accusing the judges of holding old grudges against him. And he has been dominating the senior tennis circuit, even if the old demons still surface on court.

His TV commentary during Wimbledon and the U.S. and French Opens has won plaudits for him as the best sports announcer this side of football's John Madden. He's outspoken, smart, and funny. But even in the booth he is never too far from controversy. A few years back, he took some shots at his longtime friend Carillo, suggesting that women should not commentate on men's tennis. But he didn't stop there. "I don't know any women who know the men's game," he said at a press conference. "At the same time, I'm not sure men can really know the women's game. I mean, how would they know how women are feeling at a certain time of the month?"

It was further proof of the many contradictions within McEnroe; though he'd long been one of tennis's few progressive thinkers on race – he refused to play a $1 million exhibition in Sun City in the mid-eighties due to his opposition to apartheid – he'd often seemed like a Neanderthal when it came to women. For her part, Carillo expressed hurt and disappointment in her friend. "So much of his graceless and disappointing behavior comes from not looking beyond his own feelings," she told the *Guardian*. "Like many great artists, he has a self-destructive side."

In his biography of McEnroe, Evans reports that the actor Tom Hulce studied the behavior patterns of McEnroe while preparing for his role as Mozart in *Amadeus,* as did the great Shakespearean actor Ian McKellen for *Coriolanus.* Evans quotes a description of Coriolanus from author Peter Levi's *The Life and Times of William Shakespeare,* and, indeed, it could just as easily apply to the tennis great:

> The origin of all lay in his unsociable, supercilious and self-willed disposition, which in all cases is offensive to most people; and when combined with a passion for distinction passes into absolute savageness and mercilessness. . . . Such are the faulty parts of his character, which in all other respects is a noble one.

For more than twenty years on the public stage, John McEnroe has been unafraid, or unable, to keep suppressed the darkness most of us don't even admit to ourselves. It would be nice to believe that, as he is wont to suggest, McEnroe has, in his forties, taken solace in his family and found peace.

But there is also no denying him a sense of grudging admiration, for it takes something—a death wish? a kind of courage?—to so flagrantly parade the inner Beast, as he did June 16 on that Central Park tennis court, while Smyth and five-year-old daughter Anna looked on. And there he was in the press conference afterward, moaning about how fans at other events around the globe always cheer louder for him than they do in his hometown, conveniently glossing over the fact that, as always, he'd had the crowd—and promptly lost them by loudly proclaiming some among them to be ass-holes.

"I don't know, maybe it's my fault, I don't know," he mumbled in a monotone. Despite the flatness of tone, you could sense that, somewhere, all the old emotions were in play. Somewhere in there, John McEnroe was beating the hell out of himself.

5

No Requiem Necessary

It is as if by way of the most strenuous exigencies of the physical self, a boxer can – sometimes – transcend the merely physical. . . . . If the boxing ring is an altar, it is not an altar of sacrifice solely but one of consecration and redemption. Sometimes.

Joyce Carol Oates, *On Boxing*

HE KEEPS coming forward out of his chair, squirming away from his girlfriend as she tries to cut his hair, inching his face toward the TV screen until his nose almost touches it. It's a face more recognizable for his twenty movie roles (including the warthog from hell in *Raising Arizona*) than for the fifty-two heavyweight fights that earned him the reputation of having one of the strongest chins in boxing, a face creased and scarred, with a soft pug nose that long ago lost all its cartilage.

"Look at that," he says in a gravelly Texas twang, wincing. "See how my jaw met my shoulder, and the rest of my face followed?"

On the screen, a younger Randall "Tex" Cobb is on the receiving end of a brutal sport's most brutal beating. The Houston Astrodome, 1982: Champ Larry Holmes reduces Cobb to a swollen, bloody approximation of something human, while Howard Cosell shrieks about the massacre. Somehow Cobb stands up through fifteen rounds; Cosell quits announcing boxing soon after the fight, and the sport retires fifteen-round championship bouts. Meanwhile, Cobb goes on to stake out ground on the periphery of celebrity, somewhere between star and cult figure. Though his title shot is gone, he keeps fighting while landing movie roles – *Uncommon Valor*, *The Golden Child*, and *Ace Ventura: Pet Detective* among them. He even develops an entertaining shtick about that night in Houston: "Another fifteen rounds and Holmes was mine! He couldn't take that pace!"

But now it's fifteen years later, and here Tex Cobb sits, in the decrepit Philadelphia apartment he shares with Janet, his "soul mate" – a purple-haired, tattooed alterna-rocker with a penchant for sky-blue eye shadow – and their thirteen cats. Occasionally we have to pause the VCR so Cobb can smear a brown laxative on the lips of one of them. It's ninety-five degrees outside and hotter inside – "as hot as a whore on cowboy payday," he says. As Janet fusses with his curly mane – she applies a fruity-smelling mousse and often announces in singsong baby talk that "Randall's going to have a good hair day" – he clutches a copy of the *Book of Five Rings*, the spiritual saga of Miyamoto Musashi, a Japanese warrior swordsman who sequesters himself in a cave for twenty years to deal with, and ultimately overcome, loss. Cobb sits there, burning incense despite the heat, books on Zen and spiritualism strewn throughout the room, a down-on-his-luck ex-fighter and sometime movie actor, watching his beating.

If the ring does reveal character, if something fundamental in the makeup of Mike Tyson became inescapable that summer night in Las Vegas when he gnawed on Evander Holyfield's ear, then this tape gives us Cobb. As Cosell shrieks, as Holmes tees off, not only does Cobb keep coming forward – like the warriors he reads about – he *likes* it, too.

But Cosell doesn't see the point. "Lord knows, maybe this man can stand up and take this for fifteen rounds," he whines. "What does that prove? Who knows what the after-effects will be?"

Cobb smiles. "You gonna die, Howard, that's what's gonna happen," he says. "And my greatest contribution to mankind will be retiring your sorry ass. 'Less I cure cancer."

Saying that this brutality doesn't deserve commentary, Cosell is silent. We are, too. I feel myself cringing along with Cosell, while Cobb sits, impassive. Janet asks if watching makes him sad. "No," he says, after a pause. "'Cause I gotta be the only guy to take the greatest single defeat in the history of sports and turn it into my biggest victory. Nobody ever lost fifteen of fifteen rounds. But I'm not out there just trying to survive. Look. You don't see that white boy running or hiding or grabbing. Sunshine, anyone can be a hero going downhill. The measure of a man is what happens when nothing works and you got the guts to go on. That's what Howard fucking Cosell can't see."

On the screen, a furious combination seems to cartoonishly elongate Cobb's neck. He starts shouting at this younger image of himself. "Not one step back!" he says. "Step into that buzz saw, baby! You got more ass than he got leather to kick it with!"

Finally, the fight thankfully over, a horrific image fills the screen: Randy Cobb's puffy cheeks, bloody mouth, slitted eyes. "Now watch closely," he instructs.

And there on the screen is, of all things, a smile. And then he clearly mouths two words: "Let's party."

THOSE IN boxing nod sadly when the subject comes up: damage. The damage punches do. They will tell you that boxing isn't about hitting so much as it's about being hit, and that the effects of a punch are felt on impact and then again later, when they join all the others. The effects are partly physical, partly mental. Some, like Ali, lose their faculties; others, like Jake LaMotta, seem to court the punishment to feed their self-loathing.

But the fighter who arguably took more blows to the head than any modern-day heavyweight contender – his whole game was to absorb punches until his opponent tired of throwing them – seems to defy the laws of damage. Ali has been silenced; Frazier's speech is barely discernible; Jerry Quarry floats in and out of lucidity. Yet Tex Cobb is still standing. In the fifteen years since the devastating loss that he sees as his greatest victory, he has known other kinds of losses, too: He's lost a fortune, a movie career, a chance at a boxing comeback. He's lost these things, yet in many ways in 1997 he's leading a richer life; at forty-three, he is a singular, atavistic figure who seems to predate the notion that there are psychological explanations for who we are.

LaMotta conveniently fit the accepted narrative: He subjected himself to beatings because he hated himself. But what to make of Cobb, for whom the ring is and always was a sacred shrine? In it you not only find out what you can stand, you exhibit it, and there ain't no hiding: Character is exposed before God.

No wonder, then, that Cobb has become a religious studies student at Temple University. Every time he went into the ring, like the knights of long ago who practiced virtue, he was showing the path to spiritual salvation by *practicing* character. Every time he took a combination thrown at him by the "baddest bitches breathing" – and stuck his chin out for more – he was preaching about what kind of pain is worthwhile on the road of self-discovery. It was, of course, something that was lost at the time, which is why Cosell was so puzzled that night in Houston. Who would have thought that one of sports' most eloquent philosopher-princes would be the bearer of this bruised, menacing countenance?

We live during a time when our sports stars are all too eager to cheerlead for God. Never mind that their loud, clichéd pronouncements actually call into question the depth of their faith; they inundate us with tales of divine intervention on our fields of play. Minutes after the 1997 Sugar Bowl, for instance, there was University of Florida quarterback Danny Wuerffel, crediting his performance to his "Lord and Savior, Jesus Christ." (Apparently, deities throw some mean-ass blocks.) And when the NFL's Reggie White was weighing offers as a free agent, he announced that "Jesus will make my decision for me." Lo and behold, Jesus, that noted capitalist, opted for Green Bay – the highest bidder.

Cobb's spirituality, by contrast, is nonverbal; he doesn't do Godspeak. He will quip, however, that he's back in school because "after thirty years of getting hit in the mouth, you'd be looking for God too." And when pushed, he'll say, "I'm not going to bore you with how often I read the Bible, because it ain't about what you say, Sunshine; it's about what you do."

Yet, when someone comes along and notices what he stands for, the moral covenant he has made, he is willing to have himself explained. Little wonder, then, about his close relationship in the late seventies and early eighties with writer Pete Dexter, who, while writing a column for the *Philadelphia Daily News*, became Cobb's Boswell. (Dexter, whose life was saved by Cobb in an infamous barroom brawl, went on to win a National Book Award for *Paris Trout* and become a Hollywood screenwriter.)

It also explains why, when Joyce Carol Oates recently passed through town on a book tour, Cobb sought her out and asked her to define "heart." She said it is the X factor and cited Ali, Sugar Ray Leonard, and Cobb as possessors of it. A puzzled Cobb came away unconvinced that "she gets it." And that's why my phone will ring late at night, and it will be Cobb's gruff growl or maniacal laugh at the other end – *Aah! Aah! Aah! Aah!* – and he'll tell me to meet him at the gym, there's something he wants to show me, and I will go and watch him take punches while he doesn't say a word.

What he's showing me, of course, is the heart of a warrior, something boxing aficionados can smell – who has it, who pretends. And watching the display makes you look into yourself and face the fact that whatever the endeavor, quitting has almost always been the easiest and most settled-on option. "This guy is an unbelievable warrior," shouted Sugar Ray Leonard during one of Cobb's two wars against Michael Dokes. "He'd fight King Kong if you asked him to."

And the lifelong apprenticeship in warriorship continues. It began after his dad died, when Randy was six and got his first lesson in heart: watching his mother, Norma – "the greatest American to ever breathe air and have breasts" – raise four boys by working three jobs. But it wasn't until 1974, when he was twenty, that Cobb decided to live his life as though he were starring in his own movie. The film *Billy Jack* inspired him to walk away from a football scholarship at Abilene Christian University, where he was an offensive lineman for future NFL running back Wilbert Montgomery. Cobb was, in his own words, "young, dumb, full of cum, and willing to fight everybody some." Already a black belt in karate (he would later fight for a world kickboxing title and lose a controversial decision), Cobb took off cross-country on a motorcycle, fighting local ninja deadlies from Omaha to Albuquerque. Like *Billy Jack*, it was more than the rambunctious yearnings of youth; even then he was on a spiritual quest that went well beyond tough-guy posturing. "You watch me in the ring, in the dojo, or on my street corner," he says. "I don't just stand there. I come at it."

But then, while Cobb was on the comeback trail four years ago, *Sports Illustrated* lobbed a charge of fight fixing his way, and he returned to Philadelphia, his adopted hometown. Suddenly, the only way he had ever defined himself—as a righteous warrior, just like Billy Jack—was called into question. "I have a life based on the principles of Christ, but I ain't talking about Christianity, Protestantism, Catholicism, or Judaism, Sunshine," he says, grudgingly giving voice to the spirituality he prefers to embody. "I don't believe much in team colors. What I know is that God sees the heart of a man. What I know is what I've shown. Character, that's what God and the angels know about you. Reputation, that's what men think of you. I'll live with what God knows."

TEX COBB was once the baddest-assed white boy in Philly, fighting out of Joe Frazier's gym back in the late seventies. He returned three years ago, penniless and dependent on the kindness of longtime friends, who ponied up money for the apartment and who have treated him to meals and wheels ever since.

The boxing money went to what he calls his "fearless management," a couple of hucksters who promised him millions. What he got instead was liabilities; when the IRS sought $226,000 in taxes for his $100,000 cut of the Holmes fight, Cobb knew he'd been had. (When he beat Leon Spinks in 1988, the government garnished his $25,000 paycheck twenty minutes after the fight.) Then there are the two ex-wives, not to mention the Hollywood years in the mid-eighties, when what he didn't give away went up the very nose that had taken a different kind of punishment for so long.

But truth be told, like any true believer, Cobb has never cared about the money. Even before the Holmes fight, he had suspicions about his managers, Joe Gramby and Paul Clinite, both now deceased. But he thought he could make more money than anyone could take. Besides, early on Clinite had wired Norma $2,000 to pay for her gallbladder operation. "He bought himself a white boy when he helped out my mama," Cobb says. Clinite, in particular, became a father figure, but once the depth of his treachery became apparent, Cobb says he severed all ties. He turned to his friend Joe Derrick, who also stole from him; rather than face Cobb, Derrick blew his brains out with a shotgun.

It was the betrayals that hurt, not the lost cash. Hell, it was often Cobb who was screwing himself out of money. On the eve of his 1980 fight against Ken Norton, he went so far as to bet his entire purse – about $200,000 – on himself; when he lost a split decision that many observers thought should have gone his way, he walked away without a penny, but not before trying to convince Norton to settle things *mano a mano* back at the hotel. Norton threatened to call the cops.

"I couldn't give the money away fast enough," he says now, sitting in the swelter of an apartment that in the winter has gone weeks at a time without heat. "I wasn't about the money; I was about the fight – anywhere, anytime you want to don silk and leather, Sunshine. I come to war. That's what I did."

Now he's trying to get back on his feet. Though the movies aren't his passion – he says acting is getting paid to pretend and boxing is getting paid to reveal yourself – he and good friend Willie Nelson hope to shoot a Western together. (They commiserate together about the long arm of the IRS.) And he periodically scrapes together a few bucks from appearances at gym openings or area boxing matches, where the crowds go wild for him. In fact, because he's recognized as both a boxer and an actor, he is often swarmed by autograph seekers. Cobb will have lunch with John Lucas, former coach and general manager of the Philadelphia 76ers, or sit ringside with boxer Bert Cooper, and the lines begin to form – for him. He signs every autograph request, muttering to friends under his breath, "Ain't worth two fuckin' nickels," over and over again, loving the irony.

And anytime Cobb goes near a ring, he talks excitedly about "my nipples getting hard." Part of it is the adulation heaped on him there, but mostly it is the sacredness of the arena; he has seen a lifetime of bullshit, Sunshine, and the one place where you have no choice but to show just what you're made of is there, on the canvas between the ropes, wearing silk and leather. He still dreams of fighting, only this time the way he grew up doing it – no rules. The insane chaos of ultimate fighting beckons, and he also hears that in Alaska you can get upward of $50,000 for wrestling grizzly bears.

So he spends his time working out, doing eight hundred sit-ups a day, jarring the heavy bag, sparring. Not that he doesn't have any vices left from his earlier, wilder days; much of his time is spent drinking coffee with Janet – fifty-odd cups a day. They're up until the wee hours, stalking grocery shelves for Entenmann's fat-free cookies at 3 A.M., wired on caffeine – when he doesn't have homework to do, that is.

He also meets frequently with a team of lawyers handling his libel suit against *Sports Illustrated*. In October 1993, Cobb was a year into a boxing comeback, having won ten straight fights; his promoter, the flamboyant Rick "Elvis" Parker (who has since been murdered by another fighter), was negotiating for a World Boxing Organization title shot against Tommy Morrison. For Cobb it would have been about a $750,000 payday, enough to settle some old IRS debts.

But the fight never came off – not after *SI* published a story about Parker and fight fixing that included a sidebar by the first of Cobb's opponents on the comeback trail, journeyman Sonny Barch, a blubbery blond who resembles comedian Chris Farley. Barch claimed to have been paid by Parker and Cobb to take a dive. Barch was paid $15,000 by the magazine for the story; Cobb says he has an affidavit from Barch recanting the allegation.

The day after the article hit newsstands, Old El Paso pulled a salsa commercial featuring Cobb losing a taco-eating contest to a little girl. But that doesn't bother Cobb. Nor does *SI*'s claim that Cobb tested positive for cocaine prior to the fight (a charge that was retracted in a subsequent issue). No, what bothers him is one specific line in Barch's account. Over dinner in a trendy Italian restaurant (where Cobb orders two entrées and two desserts – one each to go), I read him the line, the part where Barch hit Cobb in the fight's opening seconds and "saw real fear in Tex's eyes." I read the line, and Cobb slowly closes his eyes while Janet casts hers downward. He clenches his fists and begins talking in a voice altogether different from his normal tone, a whisper thick with violence and danger. "I've taken the best from Shavers, Holmes, Dokes, Norton, and Spinks, and I've paid this son of a bitch to go down?" he says, his eyes still closed, trying to control himself. "Ask any of them guys. They'll tell you I got only one move. They'll tell you, you ain't gonna like the way it turns out, 'cause I'm gonna break you at the knees, Baby-cakes. I'm gonna get up in your ass; I'm gonna tear your eyes out; I'm gonna chew on your Adam's apple, boy. They'll find my big butt dead up in your ass chewin' you to a bloody fuckin' stump by the time the cops get there, all right?"

He looks up at me, and, yes, I am scared. "Sure, I've been afraid; I've made a living out of fear," Cobb says, back to normal. "But afraid of getting hit in the mouth? Shit, that was an everyday occurrence. God knows I'm a fuckup, but he also knows what I know, that courage isn't the absence of fear; it's the dealing with it, darling. You ask Holmes if he saw a white boy get scared and give in. Or if he saw a cowboy with hard nipples who ain't never had enough."

"THE THING about you, Randy, is you didn't negotiate and you partied too much," Larry Holmes is saying, sitting behind a big desk in his spacious office at Larry Holmes Enterprises Inc. in Easton, Pennsylvania, about an hour outside Philly. Cobb has stopped in to say hello on his way to the fights in Allentown, where a local promoter will pay him to sit ringside, do some color commentary, and sign autographs. (When asked to plug the promoter's next card over the PA system, Cobb will bring down the house: "In a matter of weeks, there's gonna be some murder and mayhem disguised as boxing. There'll be blood, teeth, and hair flying everywhere. So bring the family.")

Fifteen years ago, Cobb and Holmes went to war against each other, and it's left a bond; they share a unique intimacy. When you've seen what each has in the other's eyes, a combination of fear and will and fire, polite niceties become superfluous. Holmes begins unburdening himself to Cobb, confessing that he's still fighting, at forty-seven, solely for the money and complaining about how his hometown has never really appreciated him, about his overhead (he has some eighty employees), about how supposed friends rush to sue him simply because he has a few bucks. Cobb, who has cause for regret, says nothing. Suddenly, it makes sense now, given Holmes's bitterness and Cobb's refusal to wallow in should-haves or could-haves, how Cobb can look at the tape of their fight and see a moral victory.

"See, I remember how it was, Randy," Holmes is saying affectionately. "You'd be like, 'A hundred grand? OK, let's go to war and then get drunk.' Right?"

They laugh. On the walls are portraits of every fighter Holmes ever fought. In one a young Randy Cobb glares at the camera. Not far away rests a photo of Gerry Cooney, the "great white hope" that Cobb always refused to be. "When I fought Cooney, it was all about race," says Holmes. "With you it was just a couple of brothers going to town."

Though Holmes was the champ, Cooney got an equal purse and the cover of *Time*. He was the media darling – a "yes, sir," "no, sir" godsend meant to return the title belt to a Caucasian waist. There was only one problem: Cooney may have had the talent, but he lacked Cobb's fire. Meanwhile, Cobb's management was trying to mold him after Cooney. He was, after all, a cowboy nicknamed "Tex" who could thump and talk – if only he could lower the volume, learn to be a little more deferential.

"That's because I was Dennis Rodman before there was any profit in it, Larry," Cobb says. "I didn't wear a dress, but I had a cowboy hat and boots and talked ugly to whoever I wanted to."

"You was a crazy old fool," Holmes says, laughing, his eyes lighting up at the memory. "Remember that press conference in Pittsburgh?"

It was the eve of Holmes's title defense against Renaldo Snipes; Cobb was on the undercard, fighting (and beating)

Bernardo Mercado. Some of the greatest black fighters in history were there. When it was Cobb's turn to speak, he said, "I just want to say what an honor it is to be here with the baddest niggers alive."

Holmes, Mercado, and the rest of those in attendance ate up this crazy cowboy's insolence. Everyone did but Snipes, who jumped out of his chair and challenged Cobb then and there. "Nobody calls me nigger!" he shouted.

Cobb coolly leaned into the microphone. "I'm sorry, Renaldo," he drawled. "I was talkin' 'bout the *bad* niggers."

Now Holmes gets up from his desk and puts his arm around Cobb as their laughter bounces off the walls. "You just didn't give a fuck – pardon my language," Holmes says, looking at Janet. "Didn't you get into a fight in a bar back then?"

He's talking about "the Night." It was 1981, when Cobb's buddy and drinking partner Dexter showed up at his door a bloody mess. Some toughs in a local taproom in a blue-collar neighborhood referred to as God's Pocket hadn't taken too kindly to a Dexter column.

Cobb had Dexter take him to the bar. On the way, a van full of black guys pulled them over. "Yo, Cobb!" one yelled. "Ali just lost to Berbick!"

All of Philly knew what that would mean: Cobb was next in line for the WBA title held by Mike Weaver, a winnable fight for the heavyweight crown. They were just blocks from the bar. The thought occurred to him that if he went on, he could jeopardize the dream – he might get arrested; he might get hurt. He went anyway.

Inside the bar, they found seven guys. Then a back door opened and a stream of at least twenty more poured in, wielding baseball bats and tire irons. Cobb looked at Dexter. "I sure hope that's the softball team," he said. Someone smashed Dexter over the head; the fight moved out into the street. Cobb ended up taking on nearly thirty guys with weapons as Dexter lay unconscious at his feet in a rapidly rising puddle of his own blood. "If he's dead, so are all of you!" Cobb roared into the night.

Dexter spent a month in the hospital; Cobb broke the ulna bone in his left hand, which runs to the elbow. Gone was the title shot; a year later would come the debacle against an invincible Holmes.

But Cobb tells Holmes none of this now. Instead, he laughs. "Yeah, I got into a fight," he says, glancing at me. "Protecting, of all people, a writer. I'll tell you, writers loved me for a while after that."

But what Cobb doesn't say – and the mere fact that he doesn't – reveals more. He doesn't tell Holmes that, with Dexter still in the hospital, he went back to the bar exactly a week later with a cast on his arm. When the door swung shut behind him, all was quiet. "That's right, it's fat old Cobb," he said. "I wanted to make sure you boys were done. 'Cause I ain't full yet." They offered to buy him a beer and served up nervous platitudes about the funny nature of misunderstandings.

Nor does he tell Holmes about how Dexter then isolated himself on an island near Seattle and went on to become a millionaire while cutting off contact with the man who saved his life. He doesn't talk about how he can't bear Janet's resentment toward Dexter. "Pete's got his own stuff to deal with," he'll say when Janet makes a remark about what the aftermath of that night revealed about the writer's character. (Dexter did not respond to a request for an interview.)

And Cobb doesn't talk about the night at the movies a couple of months back, when he and Janet went to see *Michael*.

Midway through it, they looked at each other, both recognizing the main character, the angel played by John Travolta, as Cobb. When the credits rolled, they saw that Dexter had cowritten the screenplay.

Cobb an angel? "Sunshine, not any angel," he says later. "A deeply flawed warrior angel, who, the first time you see him, he's scratching his balls and drinking a beer. Who gets in a barroom brawl, one man against a crowd. Who, when he comes up against the baddest bitch around, a bull, roars, 'Battle!' and locks horns. I left that theater knowing Pete was thinking of me."

With Holmes, though, Cobb says none of this. Instead, they trade other war stories and hug goodbye. Back in my car, Cobb shadowboxes a couple of combinations; it's fifteen years later, but like Miyamoto Musashi, he's still fixated on overcoming old losses, on showing rather than telling what he's made of. "Did you see how Larry has put on some weight?" he says. "If we did it again, he wouldn't be able to dance away from me all night. Now it would be on my terms. In tight, brawlin' in a phone booth."

HE IS AT HOME in gyms, walking the floor, giving pointers to wanna-be tough guys who've learned how to look hard by snarling at the heavy bag. On this day, a father walks by with his teenage son. "See this fella," he says, pointing as if Cobb couldn't hear. "He got hit an awful lot. But he never went down. He never went down."

Cobb offers to sign the kid's gloves. Next up is a shy, pouting towhead who can't be more than six years old. "Why'd you take that dog?" he asks.

Cobb instantly knows what he's talking about. He takes the scared kid in his lap and ever so gently explains that *Ace*

Ventura: Pet Detective was just a movie, words on paper he was paid to read. "I would never hurt anything that didn't want to hurt me first," he says, tickling the boy under the chin until a smile breaks out.

Minutes later the boy and virtually everybody else in the gym watch Tex Cobb at work. He is sparring with Pennsylvania's boxing commissioner, George Bochetto, an avid amateur and one of the benefactors footing the bill for Cobb's religious studies at Temple. Janet and I stand ringside, watching Tex time and again lead with his chin. They are wearing heavy gloves and are no doubt holding back, but the slap of Bochetto's gloves landing on Cobb's head – his self-described "slab of granite" – echoes throughout the room nonetheless. Cobb keeps his hands down, inviting the blows.

"His mama tells about when he was a little boy," Janet is saying. "He'd ask her how come all the other boys still had their daddies. And she would always tell him, 'God chose you because you could handle it.'"

I look back at Cobb, who is getting hit in the face and inching forward at the same time. Onlookers are openmouthed, probably wondering if they're witnessing some weird form of self-punishment. But as Bochetto flails at him, as the gloves kiss his cheeks and putty nose, as the gawkers stifle gasps, it's just Tex, after all, practicing taking blows, showing us and the God who chose him what kind of man he is. As the punches accumulate, Tex Cobb smiles.

6

In the Name of the Father

Days before his epic third battle against Muhammad Ali—1975's "Thrilla in Manila"—Smokin' Joe Frazier sought some fresh air on his hotel room terrace. Within moments, the barking started from down below. It was Ali. As author Mark Kram tells it, Ali had grabbed a security guard's unloaded gun and was clicking off pretend shots at his nemesis. "Go back in your hole, Gorilla!" Ali raved at Frazier. "You gonna scare the people! Come out again and I'm gonna kill ya before time!" Frazier, dumbfounded, reentered his suite, met by a group of silent visitors, some of whom had earlier seen him flip over a desk in rage after a spy had returned from an Ali press conference to report that Ali had again called him an "Uncle Tom" and mocked him by hopping around like an ape. Now Frazier looked in a mirror. "Am I a gorilla?" he asked. "Am I? He don't know how this hurts my kids."

Thirty years later, Joe Frazier still can't get Ali's voice out of his head. He walks the floor of the legendary North Philly gym that bears his name, mumbling pointers to kids who are learning how to act hard while wailing on the heavy bag. His walk is slow, fragile even. He sits at a table to start one of his set tasks for the day: While we wait for his daughter Jacqui, Joe will sit here for the next hour, signing his name, right there alongside Muhammad's, to some three hundred souvenir photos that document their wars together.

"If we could get Muhammad to sign these faster, we'd make some money," Frazier says softly, the words slurring into one another, each sentence like a continuing moan. "But you seen him sign? Like this." And now his right hand, the one with the pen, is shaking uncontrollably, and Frazier is giggling. "Daddy!" his daughter Natasha calls, scolding him; the party line leading up to this month's fight between thirty-nine-year-old Jacqui and twenty-four-year-old Laila Ali, Muhammad's daughter, is that Joe has forgiven Ali for all those long-ago slights, for the entertaining but vicious shtick that turned a people against Frazier and branded him as a symbol of American imperialism and an apologist for the war in Southeast Asia. "This has been going on too long," Joe was quoted recently as saying. "It's like we've been fighting the Vietnam War."

Yet here he is now, ignoring his daughter's plea, deviating from the script. He looks up, smiling devilishly under the brim of his ever-present black fedora; despite what Ali led a nation to believe thirty years ago, he's not a bad-looking man, though the damage done to him both inside the ring and out in his fifty-seven years makes him appear considerably older, deep circles like bruises under each eye. "People wonder why Muhammad has the problems that he do," he says, looking back down at the photo before him; it's of Joe knocking Ali down in the fifteenth round of their first fight, the one Joe won. And now he addresses that image of his vanquished nemesis. "It's because you had forty fuckin' rounds with me, Butterfly. Forty fucking rounds of Frazier."

Of course, Frazier has had his tongue thickened and slowed by those same rounds – forty-two, to be precise; he has not escaped Ali's imprint. He leans forward, studying the picture in his hands. "I know I put both his asses down," Joe says. He means both ass cheeks; in this photo, Ali's right one isn't touching the canvas. "He either on his way down or trying to get up."

Fresh from a four-mile run, Jacqui comes up behind her father, looking over his shoulder. "Oh, I like that one," she says. They linger that way for a moment, father and daughter smiling down at this vision of a triumphant Frazier standing over a fallen Ali.

She's got her father's stern countenance and square jaw. They stand together as the camera whirs around them, Jacqui straining to look deadly while Joe's eyes wander blankly until he breaks out in song. *"I found my thrill on Blueberry Hill,"* he croons, before a memory intercedes. "Butterfly tell me he God," he says. "I said, 'God, you in the wrong place tonight.'" It's a story oft-told of an exchange between the two warriors during their first battle.

"And here we are helping those Ali people again, Padre," says Jacqui. "Helping them make money again."

"God put us here to help them," Joe says.

"I'm gonna help 'em to the floor, okay?" Jacqui says, flexing her muscle. She is loquacious, unlike her dad. Back in the day, Joe let his left hook speak for him; Ali was the talker. "They gonna have to repent," she goes on. "It's gonna be a revival. Laila Ali sayin' I need to stick to radio interviews 'cause I look too much like Joe Frazier and nobody needs to see that face on television. She says she don't like my vibe. I'm like, wait 'til you check out the vibe of my left hand."

Joe looks straight ahead. "She may not got the right daddy," he says, stone-faced. "She don't look like him."

Another break from the script. "Uh-oh," Jacqui says.

JUNE 8, 2001, was supposed to have all the sentimental appeal of a Hallmark card: In upstate New York, one week before Father's Day, the daughters of Ali and Frazier are to take to the ring in a pay-per-view bout (neither side will disclose the purse) as part of the Boxing Hall of Fame's induction weekend – with the real main event taking place before the bell. The two dads, the aging rivals, would embrace for all the world to see. What a storyline: the dads forgive, the daughters fight, everyone makes money.

But some wounds run too deep to be salved by photo ops. Thirty years ago, Ali felt that Frazier represented the forces that had oppressed him. Back then, Frazier insisted on continuing to call Ali "Cassius Clay" – which Ali considered his "slave name" – and Ali called Frazier an Uncle Tom, ugly and dumb. Frazier bore the collateral damage of a brilliant and often vicious wit intent on making larger, more incendiary points.

Is it any wonder, then, that here is Frazier today, chafing against the feel-good, made-for-TV ending this month, still haunted by the man to whom he is forever linked? As the years have progressed, as Ali's image has seemed to rise to near sainthood, Frazier's bitterness has only grown deeper. In 1988, five former heavyweight titleholders gathered for a promotion in a Vegas gym – Ali, Frazier, Larry Holmes, George Foreman, and Ken Norton. Ali pointed to the heavy bag and slurred a challenge to Frazier: "Let's see who hits it fastest." Frazier assumed the stance and punished the bag with a flurry of hooks, grunting all the while. Ali followed by taking the same stance, mimicking a Frazier grunt, and turning to a perplexed Joe without throwing a single punch. "Wanna see it again, Joe?" he said. Frazier had been humiliated once again; for the rest of the day, the other champs shared the job of shielding Ali from a livid Frazier.

When Ali captivated a nation in 1996 and shakily lit the Olympic torch with his afflicted right arm, Frazier's resentment made headlines. "It would have been a good thing if he would have lit the torch and fallen in. If I had the chance, I would have pushed him in," he said. He called Ali a "dodge drafter," mangling the phrase, and, as he does today, took a ghoulish delight in his erstwhile opponent's condition: "He's got Joe Frazier-itis," he said.

And now comes word that Ali might be deviating from the script, too. Turns out he may not even be at the fight on June 8. "Don't that tell you all you need to know?" Jacqui says, her voice rising. "That man should be there. 'Cause this fight is a day of reckoning. It's a point of clarification. It's a point of clarification for women, for people who are older – 'cause that's who I represent. We can not only compete, we can kick butt. It's a point of clarification for people in boxing, 'cause there's this presumption that they're stupid. And it's a point of clarification in response to all that Muhammad Ali propaganda – we'll see who the righteous one really is."

Joe wanders off to give some pointers to a young boxer who, it turns out, speaks no English; he stands at the speed bag, blank-faced, while Joe mumbles instructions. Meantime, Jacqui starts in on the heavy bag, firing combinations. She's a thirty-nine-year-old mother of three, a lawyer with little over a year's experience (and a 7–0 record) inside the ring. "If you had told me I'd be boxing, I'd be, like, 'You crazy,'" she says, pounding the bag. "But me and Laila Ali, this was meant to happen."

JACQUI FRAZIER was nine years old when her father beat Muhammad Ali for the heavyweight title in the first of their three fights, on March 8, 1971, in a fight that had somehow become a referendum on the Vietnam War. Ali was a Black Nationalist, a Muslim, a conscientious objector to the war; Frazier, born a sharecropper's son in South Carolina, had said, "Politics is a little out of my line," when asked about Vietnam. When Frazier's left hook floored Ali in the fifteenth round, it was reported that none other than President Richard Nixon jumped up and down, celebrating the defeat of that "draft dodger asshole."

Back then, Jacqui heard other kids denigrate her father in the ugliest of terms, saw her brother Marvis come home from school almost every day having fought in the playground defending his dad's name. As she got older, she saw this curious conventional wisdom take hold, the belief that Ali was a man of the people – *his people* – while her father somehow was a sellout. Didn't they know that, behind the scenes, it was Joe who lobbied on Ali's behalf when Ali was banned from boxing for refusing to be drafted? That Joe gave a cash-strapped Ali $2,000 for a hotel bill – only to see Ali turn on him once the TV cameras showed up? Today, the Fraziers remain suspicious of the media – they often begin conversations with reporters by requesting money for their cooperation. And it can be traced to the distance, as Jacqui and her siblings see it, between who their father really is and the image that Ali and the media conspired to present.

But now others are starting to comment on Ali's near-saintly image. Suddenly, Jacqui Frazier's questioning of the Ali legacy is in vogue, as a chorus of voices have similarly begun to dissent from the "Ali as social force" conventional wisdom.

According to Mike Marqusee's *Redemption Song: Muhammad Ali and the Spirit of the Sixties,* the black conservative commentator Stanley Crouch praises Ali's athletic gifts but considers the fighter's stand against the Vietnam War the action "of a dupe ... not to be taken seriously." Professor Gerald Early, editor of *The Muhammad Ali Reader,* posits that Ali "hadn't a single idea in his head ... [his] reasons for not wanting to join the army were never terribly convincing." The sports columnist Stan Hochman, who was there in the late sixties and early seventies during Ali's banishment from boxing for refusing military induction, concurs. "I think Ali had only a small sense of the issues of the day and was willing to play the race card against another black man, to force people to take sides, to root for him so he could feed off their passion," Hochman wrote after the debut of 2000's gripping HBO documentary *Ali-Frazier I: One Nation ... Divisible.* "He wanted a loud, passionate cheering section, in the arena, in the nation, in the world."

And now comes the most damning Ali revisionism yet. In *Ghosts of Manila: The Fateful Blood Feud between Muhammad Ali and Joe Frazier,* author Mark Kram turns a sharp eye to what he calls the Ali myth. "Current hagiographers have tied themselves in knots trying to elevate Ali into a heroic, defiant catalyst of the anti-war movement, a beacon of black independence," writes Kram, who covered Ali during eleven years at *Sports Illustrated.* "It's a legacy that evolves from the intellectually loose sixties, from those who were in school then and now write romance history." Instead, in a fascinating narrative, Kram posits that Ali, duped by the Muslims, was a Chauncey Gardener figure, straight from the pages of Jerzy Kosinski's *Being There*: "For his every utterance, heavy breathing from the know-nothings to the trendy tasters of faux revolution. . . . Seldom has a public figure of such superficial depth been more wrongly perceived – by the right and the left." Kram makes much of the fact that Ali couldn't locate Vietnam on a map, let alone explain what the dispute was all about.

The question left hanging, then, by Jacqui Frazier, Kram, and the other dissenters: Does one need to know policy in order to become an agent of political change? At the time, another pop culture poet of the sixties was nasally crooning that "you don't need a weatherman to know which way the wind blows"; somehow, Ali sensed something, and he navigated swirling cultural winds to end up inspiring millions by coming to symbolize political truths even he, a simple boxer, might not have fully grasped.

Like so many of those who opposed the Vietnam War, Ali's motives were, at first, personal. As Kram shows, he didn't want to die at war, and he didn't trust that, like Joe Louis during World War II, the army would use him only as a kind of goodwill ambassador, keeping him far from harm's way.

America's presence in Vietnam was still popular in February 1966, when the then-heavyweight champion was reclassified 1-A, fit for combat, by the Louisville draft board. In Miami, Ali was baffled. "Why me? I don't understand it," he said. The *New York Times'* Robert Lipsyte spent the day with a disoriented Ali and chronicled how Ali finally blurted out what would live on as perhaps the most pithy of all anti-war expressions, at a time when few dared oppose the war: "Man, I ain't got no quarrel with them Vietcong."

Lipsyte presents the statement as off-the-cuff, a visceral reaction from a confused young man. Kram maintains that the line was "slyly dropped into his presentation by Leon X, an early Muslim watchdog and headbanger." Whether impromptu or coached (do speechwriters invalidate authenticity?), it was the beginning of Ali's political awakening, one that would grow to take on internationalist proportions by the time the Supreme Court ruled in his favor in 1971.

But it was a gradual process. Ali was still confused and troubled in the late summer of 1966, when the photographer and filmmaker Gordon Parks accompanied him through the Miami ghetto for a September issue of *Life* magazine. But he was clearly basking in his newfound inner-city popularity, a feeling that would inform his burgeoning radicalism. On the street, fans flocked to him, shouting their support. "These people like me around when they got trouble," he told Parks. "Joe Louis and Sammy Davis and other Negro bigwigs don't do that. Too busy cocktailin' with the whites. I don't need bodyguards. You don't need protection from people who *love* you."

Shortly thereafter, Ali's global worldview expanded when, while in Great Britain to fight Henry Cooper, he befriended Michael X, Britain's torchbearer for Black Power. Michael X was widely portrayed in the British press as a hate-monger, but that didn't stop Ali from accompanying him to meetings with community activists. It was a stunning alliance, made all the more stark within the next year, when Michael X was first prosecuted for inciting racial hatred and then hanged in Trinidad for murder.

Back in the States, Ali was convicted in June 1967 by an all-white jury for draft evasion, which carried a five-year sentence. By now, the anti-war movement was picking up steam – though polls still showed most Americans supported the war – and Ali spoke to his first and only anti-war demonstration in Los Angeles. "Anything designed for peace and to stop the killing I'm for one hundred percent," he said. "I'm not a leader. I'm not here to advise you. But I encourage you to express yourself."

By the late sixties, many black athletes had followed Ali and spoken out, including football's Jim Brown, basketball's Bill Russell, and track and field's Tommie Smith and John Carlos. But Ali continued to lead the sports world in radicalism. When *Esquire* magazine gave him five pages to do with what he would, he crafted (or, as Kram would suggest, had crafted for him) a political manifesto: "[Black athletes should] take all this fame the white man gave to us because we fought for his entertainment, and we can turn it around," he wrote. "Instead of beating up each other . . . we will use our fame for freedom." He went on to make the case for reparations, long before the term ever entered the Zeitgeist, suggesting we take $25 billion earmarked for the war and instead build homes in Georgia, Mississippi, and Alabama. "Each black man who needs it is going to be given a home," he wrote. "Now, black people, we're not repaying you. We ain't giving you nothing. We're guilty. We owe it to you."

By the time of Ali's 1970 interview in the *Black Scholar*, it's impossible to deny that he'd become a full-fledged revolutionary. "I was determined to be one nigger that the white man didn't get," he said. "Go on and join something. If it isn't the Muslims, at least join the Black Panthers. Join something bad. . . . I hate to see black women and men, once they get prestige and greatness, where they can go into ghettos and pick up little black babies and make them feel good, to go leave and marry somebody else and put the money in that race. . . . Now the white man's got the heavyweight champion – Joe Frazier's got a white girlfriend."

Seen in the context of Ali's evolution, could it be that, to Ali, such taunting of Frazier wasn't just the mean-spirited nastiness we see it for today? That it was also political? There is no excuse for the way Ali belittled Frazier; but could it be that Ali saw Frazier – "politics is a little out of my line" – as a stand-in for his oppressors?

"Joe, in his innocence, was representing white America – in his innocence," says football great–turned–activist Jim Brown in last year's HBO documentary. "And that will incense a revolutionary who is trying to make change and knows doggone well there's no equality."

In the final analysis, to subscribe to the revisionism of Kram, Early, Crouch, and Hochman, among others, is to argue from a privileged point of hindsight, to ignore the circumstances of the day in which Ali reigned. As Marqusee points out, from 1967 to 1970, Ali had every reason to believe that, if he persisted in refusing induction, he'd not only never fight again – he'd go to jail. After all, had a prominent black man yet stood up to the U.S. government without paying a price? Paul Robeson hadn't, nor had W. E. B. Du Bois. And yet Ali forged ahead, even when facing five years in jail. Despite the fact that, yes, he treated Frazier unfairly.

JACQUI FRAZIER will have none of it. She has a score to settle, and it has nothing to do with what went on inside the ring between her dad and Laila Ali's father. No, to Jacqui, she is on a mission to recapture her father's identity as a black man in America.

"No one knows Joe Frazier," Jacqui says now, while gym regulars float past and offer best wishes to "Sister Smoke." "People wanted him isolated. You know, it's like with a kid. If

I want to molest you, I'm gonna isolate you. My father was isolated, by Ali, by the media, by the people that were backing him – they wanted him to be this fighter they could rip off, like all the other fighters, like Joe Louis and Jack Johnson. So what they did, like with women, they put my father in a position where they make him an object, you know? That way, when some people want to rape you, it's okay because it's not really a person there, it's an object."

Joe taught Marvis and his brothers to box, Jacqui says, the minute they could raise their arms. But not her. "He always told my brothers to look out for me, to protect me," she recalls. "That's one of the reasons I'm doing this, now. What about the little girls, when they don't have a brother around, and somebody is trying to take their pocketbook or something more valuable than that? We teach our daughters to wear the skirt and put on the lipstick, but girls can be tough. Let me tell you right now, delivering a baby is more brutal than getting in the ring. You gotta go through nine months and then a real dramatic ending to get this tremendous gift you gonna have to discipline for the rest of your life – that ain't some damned cakewalk."

Jacqui swears she never gave a thought to boxing before a reporter called, telling her that Laila Ali had just won her first pro fight. And then Jacqui, the not-so-silent Frazier, opened her big mouth: "I'll kick her butt," she said, and it went out on the news wires as a front-page challenge. At the supermarket, someone asked if she was serious. "You think I'd play games with my father's legacy?" she responded.

"That's when I said, damn, she's gonna do this," recalls Peter Lyde, Jacqui's husband and manager. At the time, the 5'9" Jacqui weighed 210 pounds – about 46 more than she does now. Joe didn't like the idea of her boxing; in fact, both he and Ali (and George Foreman, whose daughter, Carla, has also turned pro) discouraged their daughters. "He didn't say it, but I could tell he was thinking, 'Well, at least it'll get her fat butt in shape,'" says Jacqui.

"You don't tell your kids who to love," Joe says. "They do what they want. I said no and she said, 'Daddy, I wanna.' But Jackie musta want this for a long time and never said nothing. 'Cause she love it."

Still, Laila Ali is widely favored. She's younger, more in shape. But Jacqui's not hearing it. She's shadowboxing in the ring, crouching down in the peek-a-boo style of her dad, uncoiling phantom left hooks. Her trash talk may sound like it's borrowed from a WWF telecast, but then again, Ali, ever the showman, presaged wrestling's huge popularity – and Jacqui's nonstop rhetoric makes its own kind of sense.

"My job is not to have mercy on her, okay?" Jacqui is saying. "Write this down. That's up to the good Lord, okay? Everything comes in threes, you know, and we're fighting thirty years and three months from the time our daddies first fought. I pray the good Lord has mercy on her."

As Jacqui continues her verbal assault on the daughter of Muhammad Ali, her husband walks by and breaks into a smile. "She's already in Laila's head. Laila don't know what to do," Peter Lyde says. "Jacqui's pulling a role reversal."

7

The Unloved

Beyond all the years of practice and all the hours of glory waits the inexorable terror of living without the game.

Senator Bill Bradley, former New York Knick

A GLOVE protrudes from his right rear pocket as Michael Jack Schmidt, gazing intently at the ball, wiggles his hips in anticipation just before uncoiling a compact textbook swing. The ball isn't just struck, it's launched.

"They don't get any better than that," he says as he follows through and watches the ball's flight before it kisses the green some 250 yards away. It is six summers since Mike Schmidt last watched the trajectory of a slightly larger ball after a similarly expert swing; six summers since the best third baseman baseball's ever known walked away from the game; six summers into a new life, one that seems more like a state of exile than retirement.

"You find yourself a retired person at the age of thirty-nine, and for five years before that you were told by everyone, 'Whatever you want to do after you retire, you can do,'" he says, walking after his ball on the tenth hole of the exclusive Medalist Golf Club's course, codesigned by pro golfer Greg

107

Norman. This is where Schmidt can be found most days, working alone on his game, harboring vague hopes of joining the PGA Senior Tour when he turns fifty in 1999. "You start believing there's always going to be something for you. Then you retire, and you're puttering around the house and the phone isn't ringing."

Since moving to Jupiter, Florida, three years ago, Schmidt has settled into a comfortable routine – he lives on the water, owns a boat and a boating business, coaches for his son's high school baseball team, and works on his golf game. His ties to Philadelphia are tenuous; he and his wife, Donna, a South Philly native, return occasionally to visit her family, and he's an investor in a chain of hoagie shops bearing his name. He says he's happy now – "Where else can I just show up and have Greg Norman or Nick Price, two of the best golfers in the world, come over and ask if I've got a game?" – but, as he prepares for his career's consummate honor at Cooperstown in July of 1995, it's clear Mike Schmidt is haunted by the life that preceded this middle age, still scarred by the invective that assaulted him on countless summer nights inside the Vet, still wounded by the Phillies' refusal to find a place for him in the organization, still smarting from the by-now-familiar raps on his game popularized by an often cynical press.

As he expertly whacks a golf ball with a smooth, easy swing on this gorgeous Florida day, Mike Schmidt grows increasingly morose as he talks about his former life. "I look back on that and sometimes I think it all happened to another person," he says, frowning. "You know, it's hard for me to be positive, to have real good things to say about a town that never did anything for me and in general made life miserable for me."

You wonder what it would take to bring Mike Schmidt a sense of contentment. He runs his hand through his thick, graying hair. He sighs and looks down, preparing to smack yet another ball. "I've never understood the concept of peace," he says.

IT WAS ABOUT seven o'clock one morning during the winter following the 1983 World Series, the one in which Schmidt had managed just one bloop single in twenty at-bats as the Phillies lost in five games to the Baltimore Orioles. It had been snowing most of the night, so Schmidt wasn't surprised when the phone rang and he learned that the school bus carrying the kids – Jonathan and Jessica – had gotten stuck. He got in his four-wheel drive and braved the slick suburban streets around Media, Pa., before pulling up alongside a yellow bus on the side of the road. Rolling down the window, he realized it wasn't his kids'.

"I saw all these cute grade-schoolers on the bus," he recalls today, sitting behind the wheel of his emerald-green Lexus on his way to pick up Jonathan, now fifteen, from school. "All of a sudden, one of these really cute kids recognizes me – I see him point and yell. They must have been in fourth grade. Then the whole damn bus, every one of these kids, just starts booing me."

Schmidt winces at the memory. I can't help but laugh at the image. "You think that's funny?" he asks pointedly. "I'll never forget that. I think it's sickening."

This is what comes to Mike Schmidt's mind when he is asked about his painful relationship with the Philadelphia fans. Over the years, as Schmidt is quick to point out, many athletes have been driven from this town by the fanatics whose idea of rooting is to hurl obscenities at the guys they cheer with equal passion the moment a game-winning homer is hit or shot sunk. Was there anything more hypocritical than the way, after Schmidt's five hundredth home run, the fans started cheering him? Even that was done grudgingly. He even had the insult of watching his Center City restaurant, Michael Jack's, go belly-up.

Of course, he's not alone. The list of those athletes happy to escape Philly's antipathy reads like an all-time all-star team: Wilt Chamberlain, Dick Allen, Del Ennis, Charles Barkley. But Schmidt, the most accomplished jock Philadelphia's ever had, may have gotten the worst of it. Yes, despite the home runs, the MVPs, the Gold Gloves, Mike Schmidt's real legacy may lie in what his treatment says about Philly sports fans – that we're not as discerning or sophisticated as we think, that excellence isn't enough for us. He is a symbol of our shame, the Philly fan's Scarlet Letter.

"Forget about his dominance of the eighties – just look at what he did in the seventies," says sportscaster and baseball maven Bob Costas. "If he has *that* career in St. Louis [Costas's home], he's probably a god. For fans who pride themselves on their baseball smarts, it's a mystery to me why Philadelphia never really embraced the player who is the modern era's clear-cut choice as the best to ever play a position."

Of course, the conventional wisdom, which even Schmidt subscribes to, is that he didn't fit the Philly fan's shot-and-a-beer mold. "I was not the type of player who lit the fire of the average fan in Philly," Schmidt concedes. "I may have in Los Angeles, but in Philly, they want the brawler, they want the guy who doesn't wipe the dirt off, who looks like he's having a tough time getting it done. They wanted Pete [Rose], they wanted Bobby Clarke. I'm the exact opposite."

Then again, there have been some quintessentially blue-collar types who also knew the fan's wrath – Ron Jaworski comes to mind. No, the vilification of Mike Schmidt is really about a host of complex perceptions about him – and about the essential nature of a rabid core of fans.

"They want the rest of the country to know how they are, how they treat athletes like myself," he says. "That's what they want, that's their thing. That's their release. I don't remember that city doing a lot to make me think highly of it. I mean, they've got a statue up of Julius Erving, one of my favorite people, but he didn't even play his whole career there. Look, if that's the worst thing that happens in your life – having to deal with a city like that – then you've been pretty lucky. But I don't miss the town."

Schmidt was a perfect whipping boy. Throughout his career, there were the Roses, Bowas, and Luzinskis, the scrappy overachievers, and there was Schmidt, the natural. Of course the fans would take someone like Luzinski under their wing: He looked like he lived for cheesesteaks, and he set up the Bull Ring, a section in left field for underprivileged kids. Schmidt, by contrast, never flaunted his charitable acts, and he had the ideal body for baseball along with the insouciance to convey that his on-field exploits were divinely inspired.

They weren't, not entirely. Back then, much was made of Bowa's having been cut from his high school team, but hardly anyone knew that Schmidt was a college walk-on. He'd had two knee surgeries while in high school in Dayton, Ohio, and as a result most scouts didn't think he'd last long in the majors. While countless column inches of area sports pages were devoted to Bowa's obsessive fielding of ground balls, Schmidt's intense preparation went unnoticed.

"Very few in the game worked as hard as I did, and I never got credit for that, because it went on behind the scenes and I never talked about it," he says as we idle in traffic before a drawbridge, one of Schmidt's few complaints about Florida living. "I'm talking about being consumed by the sport. Players today come to the park, watch some TV, read a newspaper, make a sandwich, have a few laughs, break out the cards, ease into their uniforms, and then it's time for batting practice. When I got to the park, I started preparing immediately. I was all business."

Schmidt was aloof, but over nearly twenty years in Philly's limelight there were no headlines recounting brushes with the law or loutish behavior in public places. Still, every time I wonder aloud to friends about the reasons behind the fans' mistreatment of Schmidt, there is a strange tendency to blame the victim: The guy was a jerk, they say, a verdict fueled by the press. When, for instance, Schmidt was elected to the Hall of Fame, *Delaware County Daily Times* columnist Bill Brown wrote a nasty piece explaining the unexplainable: why he didn't vote for Schmidt. According to Brown, Schmidt was "arrogant," "egomaniacal," and "thoughtless," a self-obsessed "man who carried a bat to his hotel room at night and studied himself in the mirror."

Today, Schmidt is still bothered by perceptions of him that he couldn't control. "Hell, you could just listen to WIP and hear some guy call in and say his son asked for an autograph and I walked away," Schmidt says. "That's like a cancer. That goes out on the airwaves one time and I don't know how many people formulate an opinion about me. The truth is, there are players who the Philly fans love who would push a kid out of their way rather than sign an autograph. I never did that. In fact, I'd feel guilty if I had to refuse to sign a ball for a kid.

"When Jonathan was playing Little League, I tried to create a policy that I wouldn't sign autographs there, because if I signed one, it would lead to a mob scene and take away from the kids playing the game. Well, one time this cute little kid was sent over to me, on a mission from his mom, and he asked me to sign his ball. And I'm sitting there trying to explain to this little kid about my policy. I told him I couldn't sign the ball, but I'd take a handshake, and I patted his head. And then I watched him walk back to his mom. Now, can you imagine what that mother said when he came back without an autograph? You know what she felt: Who the hell does Mike Schmidt think he is?"

Even when he did sign autographs, Schmidt rarely showed enthusiasm. Often he'd sign a ball or program without looking a fan in the eye. It seemed like a chore to him when, in fact, it tested his lifelong shyness. He never really warmed up. In 1985, the fans started coming around to him when he donned a wild wig during infield practice to cut the tension after he had blasted the fans in the press. They cheered – Michael Jack was finally loosening up. "But that wasn't me. I was just trying to give the fans what they wanted," he says. "Larry Anderson reached into his bag of tricks and coerced me into doing it."

Away from the stadium was no different. "Schmitty hated crowds," recalls Phillies broadcaster Chris Wheeler. "I remember this one night, Jim Kaat, Tim McCarver, Schmitty, and I had an appearance in Delaware, and then we were going to some bar in King of Prussia for a drink. On our way over, Schmitty asks, 'Are there going to be people there?'

Kitty [Kaat] was like, 'No, Mike, we'll call ahead and have them clear the place out.'"

Schmidt laughs when Wheeler's anecdote is repeated. "It's true, I'm uncomfortable when I feel people staring at me like I'm on display," he says as his son, Jonathan, thin, blond-haired, and tan, gets in the car. He's a good-looking kid wearing a T-shirt and khaki shorts who answers questions with one-word, soft-spoken replies. We're heading to Miami to watch the Phillies play the Marlins tonight, a rare return for Schmidt to a major-league ballpark. But at least in Florida he can maintain some degree of anonymity. "That's why I like living here so much. As soon as I get off an airplane in Philly, though, my heart starts pumping like crazy. Because they'll yell it out in Philly – '*Hey!! There goes Michael Jack!*' You know?"

Schmidt fiddles with the car radio, passing over his usual jazz and R&B in search of something he and Jonathan can agree on. He settles on a station that plays a lot of Joe Cocker and Crosby, Stills and Nash.

"You know, I can't help who I am. I don't have a painted-on smile, and I don't look like a real pleasant guy all the time," he says. "I'd love to be different than I am. But people forget that someone is the way he is, generally, because he had a father who was that way too. And my father was not a guy the Philly fans would have enjoyed watching. He was very unemotional."

When he played, Schmidt's unemotional nature was called "cool" at a time when the word had all sorts of implications, many of them racial. In the seventies, the Phillies were a racially segregated team in a racially segregated town, and Schmidt, with his slow, cocky swagger, tight Afro, and collection of Earth, Wind and Fire albums, was an honorary brother, hanging with Dave Cash, Dick Allen, and Garry Maddox. (Ironically, emotionalism in sports has become the province of the black athlete; now it's the white guys who are removed and repressed.) In other cities at other times, to be cool might have been an asset; New Yorkers worshiped Joe DiMaggio's classy, regal countenance in the thirties and forties, for instance. But by the seventies in Philly, a whole host of attitudes went into the way we looked at our sports stars. It's not altogether far-fetched to wonder if some of the backlash against Schmidt in a town run by Frank Rizzo had to do with a demeanor recognized, on some level, as black.

"It ain't the color, it's the game, and Mike played black," says Dick Allen, now a roving hitting instructor for the Phillies. "He could gig, man, that's what we used to say. I was proud of that Afro he wore. He was the coolest white boy I ever played with. And the sportswriters knew what was going on in the clubhouse, and the fans picked it up from them."

At the time, Schmidt sought comfort from the black players in a locker room that had become a painful place for him. Bowa and Luzinski relentlessly teased him about his strikeouts, his pockmarked complexion, his "coolness." It may have been meant as good-natured locker-room banter, but Schmidt didn't see it like that. On an almost daily basis, Dave Cash would sit with Schmidt in front of his locker, massaging the slugger's battered ego, telling him to ignore his teammates' derision and repeating, over and over, "You're the man, Mike, you're the man."

"Bowa and Luzinski were unmerciful on me back then, I sensed a lot of petty jealousy from them," Schmidt says. "I saw it as mean-spirited, no question. I found a solace from the black players, who, for some reason, took a liking to me. There was just a sensitivity there I felt very comfortable with."

Bowa smiles today when asked about his riding of Schmidt. "A lot of that was because I kept reading about this shortstop they drafted who was supposedly going to be in the majors in three years," he says. "I had to let him know he'd have to play third if he wanted to make it in the big leagues. Come to think of it, I take some credit for him getting into the Hall of Fame, because if he'd taken my job, he would have been too tired to hit all those home runs."

Today, Schmidt says, his relationship with Bowa is better than ever. But the fans were a tougher problem to overcome. Even in the eighties, the decade Schmidt won his trio of MVP awards, there were nights that, when dredged up now, still send him into deep funks. One comes to mind as we pull into Joe Robbie Stadium.

Schmidt lowers his window, telling the guard, "My name is Mike Schmidt," while Jonathan rolls his eyes – "He knows who you are, Dad." Just then, Schmidt is revisited by a painful recollection.

It's a tight game at home against the Expos in 1983. Four times Schmidt comes up and four times he strikes out on consecutive pitches. Twelve pitches, four outs. Each time, as he walks back to the dugout, the boos get louder and angrier. Finally, in extra innings, he hits pitch number thirteen off ace reliever Jeff Reardon for a game-winning home run and sprints around the bases, aware of the deafening cheers, his stomach churning. He runs past his teammates, into the dugout, down the runway to his locker, thinking about the fans, how they're not really ever with him, how they don't deserve a slow trot and don't deserve a tip of the hat – why *should* he savor the moment? – and he grabs his keys without breaking stride, sprints to the car, and then he's on his way home, in full uniform, blasting hard-driving funk music all the way.

THE PHILLIES ARE taking batting practice, and Mike Schmidt, Jonathan close by his side, is sitting in the Phils' dugout. "This is neat," Jonathan says, watching light-hitting second baseman Mickey Morandini take his cuts. "But, Dad, how come they're all trying to go yard [hit it out of the park]?"

Schmidt smiles. "Because they get paid $5 million a year, they can do whatever they want," he says. "But I can tell you this: They wouldn't be doing that if I were out there working with them."

At the end of the dugout sits Phils general manager Lee Thomas, who looks over a number of times before approaching Schmidt. When he does, Thomas's gregariousness is overwhelming. "I hear you're broadcasting a couple of games for the Baseball Network? That's *terrific,* Mike, just *terrific,*" Thomas says, pumping Schmidt's arm a little too enthusiastically.

Schmidt mumbles a thank-you and, as he walks away during the brief exchange, raises his eyebrows. "That may have been the longest conversation we've ever had," he says as we make our way to the press box. "I can understand Lee being a little nervous around me, though. Everywhere that guy goes, he must hear, 'Oh, you have Schmitty's job.' And, look, if I was hired as the general manager in St. Louis tomorrow, I don't know if the first thing I'd do is ask Stan Musial what job he'd want. But I'd also be sure he and I were on good terms and that Stan would be available if I needed him for something, whether it's teaching a minor-leaguer how to field ground balls or to do promotions."

In 1988, as his playing days were winding down, Schmidt asked Phils owner Bill Giles for the general manager's job. Four years before, Flyers owner Ed Snider promoted his superstar, Bobby Clarke, from center ice to the GM's office. Giles, who by no means considered the job Schmidt's for the taking, instead encouraged him to pursue a career in broadcasting and hired Thomas.

In 1991, a frustrated Schmidt told Ray Didinger of the *Daily News*, "Let me tell you . . . there's only one guy in this town whose organization that is, and it's mine. Somebody else may own it, but it's mine."

"I don't think that went over too well with the people who actually own the team," Schmidt says today, laughing. Looking back, he concedes he was a bit of a "lost soul" after his retirement and was hurt that the Phillies felt he should start by managing in the minor leagues, as if he needed to prove he knew the game.

A year later, though, he was ready to do just that. The Double A Reading Phils were looking for a manager. He called Del Unser, the team's director of player development, and expressed interest. "Del was my good friend," Schmidt says. "He and I had stayed up 'til four in the morning in the minor leagues in many a hotel bar, talking baseball."

Nonetheless, Unser rebuffed his former teammate. A subsequent offer by Schmidt to go to Clearwater and work with the younger players was similarly declined.

"Maybe it's not like I perceive it to be," Schmidt says, grabbing a tray and getting in the crowded press room's cafeteria line. A lot of eyes are on him and he feels it. He begins to talk softly. "When I'm around the Phillies, everybody's so nice, it's always 'How's Donna and the kids?' and everybody's all lovey-dovey. But maybe when those guys are upstairs at the Vet, thinking about the future, maybe they're saying, 'We don't want Schmidt around.' See, Bill and Lee don't see me as a guy who would go to Spartanburg for a week and live in a Holiday Inn. The problem for me is that, generally, the people who run the game are almost all fringe players, guys who weren't stars. So they think I can't relate to the normal hitter."

"I don't think Mike had the people skills to be a manager or general manager," explains Giles. "I never thought he'd make a good leader. Besides, most great players who try to become managers don't do well because the game came so easily to them."

To Schmidt, Giles' reasoning amounts to once again being labeled "a natural," which he interprets as a knock against his work ethic. "I went from ducking every time they threw a breaking ball to being the best right-handed breaking-ball hitter in the league, because I had the patience and drive to learn the game," he says. "I climbed about every fence, and people never want to give me any credit for that. Do you ever hear anybody say, 'That Mike Schmidt, he sure had baseball smarts'? They don't say that."

And yet, it was his analytical nature – not his natural talent – that was largely responsible for his Hall of Fame career. The history of baseball is littered with sluggers full of raw ability who dominate for a few years and then fade away. It wasn't so long ago, for instance, that Eric Davis was going to be the next Willie Mays. Now he's out of baseball. When Schmidt's career started to wane in the mid-eighties, it was his studied approach to the art of hitting that resurrected him. He changed his style, began hitting down on the ball, and started using the whole field.

"Early in my career, pitchers would have rather faced me with two outs, a runner on second and the game on the line than Bake McBride or big Bull Luzinski, because those guys would hit bloop singles in that situation and I'd strike out – I was trying too hard," he says. "But late in my career, I became a clutch hitter. And there's no question it was because of my desire to get into the dynamics of the swing and make adjustments. It's something Dale Murphy, for whatever reason, didn't do. But, still, you don't hear people saying, 'Boy, Schmidt would make a great coach.'"

Even now, the perception that Schmidt was not a clutch hitter persists. Wheeler says that when he speaks to area groups today, someone will invariably claim that Schmidt never drove in a big run. It's a rap that should've been dropped in 1980, when he hit four game-winning home runs during the pennant drive and was named MVP of the World Series after hitting .381. And the statistics bear out Schmidt's claim that, in the mid-eighties, he began consistently delivering in crunch time. From 1984 to 1988, his overall average was .274, but he hit twenty points higher with runners in scoring position and in "late-inning pressure situations" – any at-bat in the last three innings with runners on base and his team trailing by three or fewer runs.

Far from being a hindrance, Schmidt's penchant for analysis enabled him to become a money player. "If I had been some dumb guy, one of those guys perceived as kind of country, they'd have said I was better than I was," he says, eating a side of popcorn with his pasta entrée. "That's the perception – 'If only he had been less sensitive and a little bit ignorant, imagine how good he could have been.' And you're powerless over things like that. It's probably something some announcer said to a writer and then that shit takes on a life of its own."

It is twenty minutes to game time, and broadcaster Harry Kalas ambles over to the table, intoning , *"Michael Jack, how ya hitting 'em?"* and asking Jonathan what *he* hit during his recent high school season. Jonathan, barely audible, replies, ".333." "He was two for six," Schmidt says, smiling, looking at his son. "Sorry, I had to tell him. You can tell I'm not *head* coach, or else he would have had twenty-five at-bats."

Kalas laughs and invites Schmidt up to the TV booth to broadcast a few innings. (In 1991, Schmidt did color commentary on PRISM's Phillies telecasts; the team's brass, however, felt he was too critical.) Before going, Schmidt turns to me. "Baseball is what I know," he says, looking at Jonathan and breaking into a grin. "I have this reservoir of knowledge, but I'm coaching kids who can't turn a double play. I'm talking to them about the dynamics of the swing, so they can go 0 for 4. But that's okay, because I'm teaching the game."

"I WANT TO SEE some homework being done back there," Schmidt says, looking in his rearview mirror. Then, turning to me, he says, "If I were as hard on my kids as I want to be, they'd probably hate me. I'm not nearly as hard on them as my father was on me."

We are on the way home, and Jonathan dutifully opens his English book. Tomorrow morning, he will begin his day by eagerly turning to the sports section, where he will dissect the Phillies box score. But his father won't. The only sport Mike Schmidt goes out of his way to watch is golf; he hardly ever watches major league baseball, even on TV. It's not because he's lost his passion for the game. It's because the game has lost its passion for him.

It's been a long, emotional day for Schmidt, talking about his former life, opening up old wounds normally salved by his nine irons or his kids' needs. What do you do when, for well over a decade, you were the best in the world at what you did – yet felt unappreciated all the while? What if the one thing you were meant to do – punish baseballs – brought you more pain than anything else in your life?

"You know, I've been real lucky, and I thank God for the fact that things are so great in my life right now – I get to spend time with my kids and play all the golf I want," he says softly. "So it's all worked out okay. I've accepted what happened. It's okay that the fans got on me the way they did, it's okay that the Phillies didn't hire me when I retired."

Mike Schmidt pauses. "But it would have been nice to have been wanted."

8

The Round Mound
Bids Farewell

It was a humbler, portlier, more emotional Charles Barkley who said goodbye to the sport of basketball April 19, 2000, the last day of the NBA regular season and the final night of his round-ball career, which had spanned sixteen riveting, often maddening, always dramatic years. Barkley had blown out a knee in December, playing for the Houston Rockets in Philadelphia, where his pro career began in 1984. The injury cut short his farewell tour; that night, the one-time bad boy of professional sports sobbed alone in his hotel room, so haunted was he by this final image of himself being carried off the court. Still, his depression didn't keep him from quipping wise-ass, as usual: "Now I'm just what America needs – another unemployed black man," he joked.

But, postsurgery, he still couldn't shake the vision of sports' hardest worker, a gallant overachiever, helpless. So he rehabbed the knee with an eye on the calendar and there he was on that April night, five months later, standing before a genuflecting Houston crowd that deafeningly chanted his name one final time after he'd plodded through the last seven minutes of professional basketball he'd ever play, making one of three shots. And then he took the micro-phone, and the Charles Barkley I'd gotten to know a decade ago emerged, the one behind the macho pose. "Basketball doesn't owe me anything," he said, voice quavering. "I owe everything in my life to basketball. I've been all over the world and it's all because of basketball." He paused before finishing by reminding both the fans and his younger team-mates to appreciate the moments of their shared passion, be-cause, it turns out, they're fleeting.

And with that, after hearing himself praised by his coach as the bearer of a "heart of a champion," after being pre-sented with a recliner by his teammates large enough to ac-commodate the girth of a rear end that his wife, Maureen, calls "the size of New Jersey," Barkley retired at age thirty-seven. Over the years, he'd transcended sports in the way few others have. Part raconteur, part provocateur, the bigness of his persona often overshadowed just how singular a talent he was on the court. There, he was a perennial all-star, a for-mer league MVP, one of only four players (Wilt Chamberlain, Kareem Abdul-Jabbar, and Karl Malone are the others) to have amassed more than twenty thousand points, ten thou-sand rebounds, and four thousand assists.

What's so startling about the numbers is another number: his height of 6'4". Though nearly a foot shorter than the bruising behemoths he battled under the boards, Barkley often dominated because of effort and will. Always a brag-gart in the showy style of his hero, Muhammad Ali, it was the incongruity between his style of play and his height that once led Barkley to declare himself "the ninth wonder of the world."

Off the court, where he spun quotes and welcomed con-troversy, Barkley was arguably the most interesting and in-fluential athlete of his time – maybe since Ali. While others packaged themselves as if they were just another product to be hawked in America's ever-burgeoning commodity culture, Barkley eschewed marketing for authenticity, giving rise to a whole generation of athletes – the hip-hoppers – for whom the ethic of "keeping it real" has become a mantra.

In recent years, Barkley has ruminated publicly about one day running for governor of his home state of Alabama. Yet when I saw him last year, such grandiose plans were far from his mind. He was typically candid when asked what he was going to do when that April night finally arrived and his career came to a close. "I want to learn to play the piano, finish college, and get really, really, really fat," he'd said.

CHARLES WADE BARKLEY was born February 20, 1963, in the small industrial town of Leeds, Alabama. His father bolted early on, and Barkley was raised by his mother, Charcey Glenn, who cleaned white people's homes, and his grandmother, Johnnie Mae Edwards, who worked in a meat factory. Later, Barkley would become the first athlete since Ali and Bill Russell to question the predominantly white sports media's insistence on conferring "role model" stature on young black athletes who conduct themselves deferentially, and, after arguing that parents and teachers should be role models, he'd always point out his: "My mother and grandmother were two of the hardest-working ladies in the world, and they raised me to work hard," he'd say. Barkley was not an athletic prodigy. He was, by all accounts, a shy, fat kid. Yet he always harbored a brash ambition. In tenth grade, pudgy and merely 5'10", he failed to make his high school varsity squad. Still, he insisted to anyone who would listen that he was going to play in the NBA. He shot baskets every night, sometimes all night (if he could escape his grandma's strict, watchful eye), and cultivated his leaping skills by repeatedly jumping back and forth over a four-foot chain-link fence.

A six-inch growth spurt his senior year led to a scholar-ship at Auburn University, where he became known as "Boy Gorge" and "the Round Mound of Rebound." At 6'4" and close to three hundred pounds, he'd rumble the length of the floor, a one-man herd, dribbling behind his back, while taller, more sculpted opponents ran for cover.

The Barkley who was drafted fifth in the 1984 NBA draft by the Philadelphia 76ers bears little resemblance to the confident public man who addressed that Houston crowd in April 2000. Joining legends Julius "Dr. J" Erving and Moses Malone, Barkley was awed by them and by the big north-eastern city itself. Beyond going to practice and games, he rarely left his rented apartment. He even called sportswrit-ers "sir." He was thankful to be where he was, and not so sure he belonged.

"When I got drafted, I knew I had a God-given ability to rebound," Barkley recalls. "But I never averaged more than fourteen points a game in college. So I was just hoping I could score ten points and get ten rebounds a game for a few years and make some money to take care of my family." Within three years, he was leading the league in rebounding and scoring more than twenty points per game.

And Barkley was changing in other ways as well. I first got to know him in 1991, when he'd already morphed into sports' preeminent anti-hero, the flip side of Michael Jor-dan's crossover-era accommodating persona. The rap group Public Enemy had paid homage to Barkley in song ("Throw down like Barkley!" Chuck D wailed on "Bring the Noise"), seeing his in-your-face game and demeanor as the hard-wood manifestation of rap. During a game in New Jersey, a courtside heckler, yelling racial epithets, was turned on by Barkley, who promptly spit on his tormentor. Only, as he'd later describe, he didn't "get enough foam" behind the loogie, and, low and behold, he mistakenly spat on a little girl.

It was a national story, of course, and Barkley was vilified. For months previous, Barkley had been persuasively arguing that athletes shouldn't be considered role models. "A million guys can dunk a basketball in jail, should they be role models?" he'd ask, offending the sportswriter crowd who, as he saw it, demanded that he know his place and be a "credit to his race." (His argument would prompt national news when he wrote the text for his "I am not a role model" Nike commercial, a carefully worded polemic that none other than Dan Quayle called a "family-values message" for Barkley's oft-ignored call for parents and teachers to quit looking to him to "raise your kids" and instead to be role models themselves.) But with what came to be known as "the spitting incident," Barkley had indeed been found guilty of conduct unbecoming a role model.

I was a pot-smoking, ponytailed, law-school dropout at the time, a sports fan who was fascinated by Barkley's ballsy media critiques. I wrote a column in a city alternative newspaper, saying that of course Barkley ought not to have spat on someone–but he was saying some things we should hear, too.

On the day the piece ran, my phone rang; Barkley was calling to thank me and to invite me over to talk about topics nonbasketball. He was distraught about the spitting incident, shattered even, because one constant over the years has been Barkley's affinity for children. He has long been one of the nation's most generous celebrities, often focusing on children's charities, though it's always been done with one caveat: that no publicity attend his good works (a rule he finally broke last year when he gave $3 million to Alabama schools).

Children don't judge with the venom of adults, he'd explain. And it was that venom he was trying to understand then, in the fallout of the spitting incident: "I think the media demands that athletes be role models," he told me, "because there's some jealousy involved. It's as if they say, this is a young black kid playing a game for a living and making all this money, so we're going to make it tough on him. And what they're really doing is telling kids to look up to someone they can't become, because not many people can be like we are. Kids can't be like Michael Jordan."

On some level, he sensed that the media conferral of role-model status was a complex thing, that the term was often used as a racial code, not unlike "welfare queen" or "all-American." It was, after all, a label placed by an overwhelmingly white press on those black athletes who, in Barkley's words, "played the game."

Barkley grew even bolder, more in-your-face. He'd inherited leadership of the 76ers from the courtly Erving and distanced himself from what he saw as just so much kiss-ass demeanor. He began conferring with Jesse Jackson and called himself a "nineties nigga – we do what we want to do." Visits to the Philadelphia locker room were the stuff of great theater, as Barkley continued to castigate the press and a city still divided by race. "Just because you give Charles Barkley a lot of money, it doesn't mean I'm not going to voice my opinions. Me getting twenty rebounds ain't important. We've got people homeless on our streets and the media is crowding around my locker. It's ludicrous," he said. He called Philly a "racist city" and told the press to "kiss my black ass – even though your lips might stink." He vowed, "I'm a strong black man – I don't have to be what you want me to be," echoing an Ali line from the sixties after he read Thomas Hauser's oral history of the boxing great. When I told him I was writing a magazine profile of Erving, he dismissed the legend: "Man, I ain't got no time to talk about no Uncle Tom."

By 1992, Barkley was the NBA's second-best player, behind Jordan, but he'd grown frustrated with Philadelphia's management for surrounding him with a rotating cast of mediocre players. Management, in turn, had tired of Barkley's outspokenness. He was traded to the Phoenix Suns, and the night before he went west, my phone rang. It was Charles, calling to thank me for leaving him a copy of *The Autobiography of Malcolm X,* about whom we'd been talking. He sounded pensive, even glum. "I'm just driving around thinking," he said. "This has been my home for eight years. I don't know what to expect somewhere else." His voice, barely a whisper, made him sound vulnerable. Oh yeah, I remember thinking, he's still in his twenties.

It was further proof that, for all his loudmouth faults, Barkley often exhibited a greater potential for growth than any other athlete on the public scene. Yet his authenticity rarely broke through the media caricature. In the soap opera narrative of sports, Barkley's "badness" was set against Jordan's "goodness," and there was little room for the complicated, three-dimensional Charles I was privy to. I'd seen the sensitive Charles, the one who teared up when talking about his younger brother, who had had a tough time with his older sibling's fame and fortune and who suffered a stroke due to cocaine abuse.

Then there was the jokester Charles, who proposed to Maureen over dinner at a nearby restaurant by having their favorite waiter actually pop the question. There was the self-deprecating Charles, who, one day, warmly lifted up a five-year-old autograph seeker, prompting her to burst into tears. "Girl, you gonna regret this someday – I'm an international sex symbol!" he said, before tickling under her chin, determined to coax a smile.

And, as always, there was the Charles who grew in the most public of ways, thanks to an insistence on engaging the world beyond the orbit of his own celebrity. He was always in a state of becoming. His iconoclasm was on display in 1988, when he told his mother he was considering voting for George Bush. "But, Charles, Bush is only for the rich," she said. "Mom, I *am* the rich," he replied. Or, three years later, when his friend Magic Johnson tested HIV positive and other players, such as Karl Malone, were calling for uniform testing in the NBA, Barkley simply stated: "I'm disappointed in myself that I haven't felt the same compassion for other people stricken with AIDS that I now feel for Magic."

In Phoenix, Barkley became a superstar. He was the league's MVP and took his Suns to the NBA Finals in 1993, where they lost to Jordan's Chicago Bulls in six hotly contested games – arguably the toughest challenge to Jordan's dominance in six championship seasons. On court, basketball fans finally saw that Barkley was the consummate team player; his five assists per game, often eye-popping behind-the-back passes while double-teamed, gave lie to the conventional wisdom that permeated his last years in Philadelphia: that he was a talented player who couldn't make his teammates better.

Off the court, Barkley continued to evolve. He entered a Republican makeover phase. His worldview began to mature; he became more focused on class and less virulent on race. He also grew close to Rush Limbaugh and Dan Quayle (a frequent golf partner), dined with Clarence Thomas, and endorsed Steve Forbes in the presidential primary. (Lucky for me he outgrew the Reverend Jackson's mentoring; at the behest of his wife, Maureen, I had an uncanny impressionist leave a series of late-night, drunken, subtly homoerotic messages for Charles from Jesse – "What would Charles Barkley look like without the uniform on?" the "Reverend" intoned in his singular cadence. Maureen found a note in Barkley's handwriting, reminding himself to "return Rev. Jackson's call.")

Though exit polls showed that his imprimatur sealed Forbes's primary win in Arizona in 1996, Barkley didn't necessarily sign on to any particular ideology. He became impossible to pigeonhole. He'd regularly lambaste liberalism, to the proud applause of Limbaugh and Quayle, saying, "Welfare gave the black man an inferiority complex. They gave us some fish instead of teaching us how to fish." In the next breath, though, he'd skewer 1994's Republican revolution as "mean-spirited" and denounce Pat Buchanan as a "neo-Nazi." A junkie of CNN's political gabfest *Crossfire*, Barkley became convinced, after reading Jonathon Kozol's *Savage Inequalities*, that the way we fund public schools – through local property taxes – is designed to produce good schools in good neighborhoods and run-down schools in run-down areas. "My daughter goes to a private school because I can afford it," he once told me, giving voice to his natural inclination toward populism. "But shouldn't everyone have great education available to them?"

He may read about failing schools, but Barkley hasn't exactly become a nerdy policy wonk. Throughout his time on the public stage, he's reveled in his fame, as when he had a brief, much-publicized tryst with Madonna, prior to a reconciliation with Maureen. Then, as now, he insisted on livin' large: "We ain't here for a long time, we here to have a good time," he often says.

Indeed, while Jordan became a reclusive prisoner to his iconic status, Barkley lived to be out among the masses, and his nightclub hopping led to more than one *mano a mano* face-off with loudmouth fans. "Let there be no conflict in America," Barkley said in 1997 after he tossed an obnoxious heckler through a plate-glass window in an Orlando, Florida, bar. "If you bother me, I whup yo' ass." His career has been dotted with such run-ins; they are the collateral damage of a personality that, as on the court, simply plows ahead, rarely stopping to consider each and every move.

Barkley never made it back to the Finals. His body had been badly beaten through so many years of manhandling by bigger players, not to mention the ill effects of his legendary hard-drinking late nights. When it got out that the Suns were fielding trade offers for him in 1996, he exploded: "The days of cotton picking are over," he told the Phoenix media. "They disrespected me by shopping me around like a piece of meat."

Traded to the Rockets, Barkley joined two other aging superstars, Hakeem Olajuwon and Clyde Drexler. They already had their championship rings and didn't seem as committed as Barkley, who cut down on his drinking, started lifting weights, and even offered to come off the bench for the good of the team in the 1997–98 season. But he was a shadow of his former self. "I'm the artist formerly known as Barkley now," he told me in 1998. "Once in a while, I get flashbacks." Indeed, his self-analysis was typically blunt. "I'm still a good player, not a great player," he said. "I can score fifteen points and get ten rebounds."

Yet the ceaseless questions about never having won a title carried the implication that he'll be remembered as less of a winner than his more hallowed contemporaries. He began to think of himself in relation to those who have won rings. "I've never played with a great player in his prime while I've been in my prime," he said. "Michael has had Scottie [Pippen]. Bird had Kevin [McHale] and Robert Parish. And Magic, shit, Magic had everybody. When I came into the league, Doc and Moses were winding down. And Hakeem and Clyde, same thing."

Toward the end, when he was seen as merely a good player, it became easy to forget what the younger Barkley once was. More than a great player, he was, like Jordan, a wonder on the court: You'd watch and not quite believe it. He was a jumping jack who was too quick for other power forwards, too strong for small forwards, and too visionary a passer for the double-team. And it was all done with an in-the-moment passion missing from today's scowling, dour-faced jocks.

Off the court, ironically, Barkley became the league's elder statesman these last few years, a respected spokesperson for tradition and the status quo. At times he'd sound like Paul Lynde from *Bye Bye Birdie,* wringing his hands over "these kids today." When it was written that the corn-rowed, tattooed Allen Iverson travels with his "posse" – friends from back home – Barkley admonished him: "Your teammates should be your posse." When I offered that guys like Iverson see the league's crackdown on droopy uniform shorts as a sign of hostility toward black culture, he demurred: "They're wrong," he said. "The shorts now are getting to the point where they don't even look like shorts. I think the NBA has to be concerned with a lot of black guys getting arrested, me included, doing drugs, wearing shorts down to their ankles. That's not hostility to black culture. That's just reality."

Still, though the volume came down a bit, Barkley continued throughout his final years as a player to challenge the predilections and prejudices of the men who present him to the world. He calls the journalistic pack "flies" because they're always buzzing around, annoying players. One day, in front of his locker, I witnessed pure Barkley. Before the throng could lob its first question at him, Barkley singled out a Houston television reporter. "Would you suck a cock for a million dollars?" he asked. A roomful of men all instantly looked at their shoes.

"No," came the cracked-voice reply.

"A billion?" Barkley challenged.

"No," said the reporter, stronger now.

"Well, how much then?"

"I wouldn't do it for anything!"

Barkley grinned widely. "Well if you'd do it for free, come on over then," he said, while nervous laughter filled the air around him. "Tell y'all what, I would. If I was poor, I'd suck a cock for a million dollars."

He paused and looked at his audience. "And y'all mutha-fuckas would do the same, you just scared to admit it," he said. "Like, remember when that movie *Indecent Proposal* came out? Oprah had on three couples who said they wouldn't let their husband or wife sleep with someone for a million dollars. Couldn't help but notice that they had money already."

After an awkward moment of silence, the flies started buzzing again, shouting basketball questions over one another's still trembling voices. I remember standing there, feeling lucky as hell to have been a witness to Barkley's unique brand of performance art. After all, anyone who appears so utterly joyous exercising free speech, anyone so okay with his life as a very public work-in-progress, and anyone in the insular, often homophobic world of jockdom who points out class distinctions by challenging the media to perform fellatio, well, that's a role model worthy of emulation.

THREE

The Entrepreneurs

9

The Graying of Dr. J

JULIUS ERVING rises from behind his cluttered desk and moves slowly about his office. Sighing, he plops down onto one of the three chairs normally reserved for guests of the Erving Group, Inc. He methodically removes his shoes and places his size 15-Ds on the coffee table in front of him.

"You never get caught up around here," he says, eyeing the pile of paperwork on his desk. "It's like being a housewife. You clean up, they come home and dirty up again, so the next day you clean up. If somebody asks you why you're cleaning up, you answer, 'So things can get dirty again.'"

Erving pauses and then breaks into a wide grin. "Now, be careful with that quote," he cautions, ever image-conscious.

Throughout his time in the public eye, Julius Erving has always tried to say the right thing, while rarely offering glimpses beneath the surface of his legend. Erving came along in the pre–Magic Johnson, pre–Michael Jordan era, when black basketball players – and the entire NBA – had an image problem, and he was the model of propriety. The creativity and spontaneity of his game were surpassed by no one. Yet, off the court, no one was more fiercely self-controlled. He seemed intent on being perceived as a positive role model while so many other stars were checking into drug rehab. During the 1987 parade down Market Street that honored him when he retired, Erving once again came up with the right words: "I didn't hear that there was no school today," he said into the microphone after noticing a sea of young faces in the crowd. "After the ceremony, get back to the classroom and take a note from the Doctor."

Since that day, Erving's public persona has been much more in keeping with his low-key side. He has retreated to the Main Line mansion he shares with his wife and four kids, commuting to his Center City office to oversee his diverse portfolio of business interests, which include part ownership of the Philadelphia Coca-Cola Bottling Company. You don't see him at 76ers games, and he doesn't appear on any talk shows. Erving goes about his business quietly – just this morning, he spoke to a small group at Thomas Jefferson University, where he awarded the Julius Erving Stipend, a cash grant, to five minority students. And for the last three hours, without fanfare or complaint, he has waded through the papers on his desk.

A decade earlier, of course, Dr. J would have been considered among the least likely Philadelphians ever to be bogged down with paperwork. But in May 1993, at age forty-three, the Julius Erving who sits in his office wearing a white turtleneck, his hair graying prematurely, has little in common with the legend of Dr. J. It is the legend who will be inducted this month into the Basketball Hall of Fame. Yet, at times, Erving says, it seems as if all the accolades and all the glory happened to someone else.

I ask him if he watched the marquee NBA matchup – Knicks-Orlando, Patrick Ewing versus Shaquille O'Neal – on

TV last night. He shakes his head. "No, I was watching *Navy Seals*" – an obscure Charlie Sheen movie. "I hadn't seen it before. I never go out of my way to watch a basketball game. If it's on when I'm flipping channels, I'll check it out, but it's never like, 'Let me stop doing what I'm doing 'cause the game's on.'"

Erving opens a can of Nordic Mist carbonated water and sees that I'm inspecting the label. "This is a Coke product," he assures me as he takes a gulp before continuing. "You've got to understand, I pledged to myself and to my family that we would not be dependent on basketball. I made a very clean break and decided not to look back."

He does, however, take a glance toward the mountain of paperwork on his desk.

IT IS, OF COURSE, a difficult transition to make. As a superstar professional athlete, you peak before thirty and "retire" soon after. In your forties, few things can replace the thrill of the sellout crowds that chanted your name two decades earlier. Mike Schmidt, for example, has yet to attain the type of personal fulfillment he found during his playing days and can often be heard blasting the Phillies for not reserving a place for him in the organization. Bobby Clarke, another one-time Philly icon, has bounced from front-office job to front-office job while publicly regretting prematurely hanging up his skates in 1984.

Early in his career, Julius Erving became determined to make a graceful transition when it was his turn to relinquish the spotlight. "There are too many athletes who have sour grapes or regrets – leaving too soon, having the career in the first place," he says. "I heard a lot of stories about Joe Louis, and it motivated me early in life. He was always used as an example of somebody who made a lot of money in his life and didn't keep it, and wound up being dependent."

Erving began thinking about life after basketball while still at the top of his game. In 1979, at the age of twenty-nine, he founded and incorporated the Erving Group and, not co-incidentally, got rid of his trademark Afro and goatee. "I had to go for that corporate business look," he says.

In fact, Erving always had business aspirations, he says. At the University of Massachusetts, he majored first in mar-keting and then in management, but his real business edu-cation started once he decided to turn pro and jump to the upstart American Basketball Association after his junior year. He came to the NBA and the 76ers in 1976 and a few years later opened a shoe store on South Street that quickly went out of business. Having to close it down stoked his com-petitive fires; Erving became determined to make it in busi-ness as he had in athletics.

Of course, he didn't starve as an athlete – in his last sea-son with the Sixers, he earned $1.49 million. Yet, today, he takes great pride in his business earnings. In addition to his Coca-Cola interest, he owns part of Garden State Cable and a Buffalo television station, sits on the board of Meridian Bank, and operates the DJ Group, Inc, the sports and enter-tainment arm of the Erving Group. (The DJ Group pro-moted the embarrassing pay-per-view one-on-one matchup between Erving and Kareem Abdul-Jabbar in Atlantic City in 1992; in 1993 the Group was producing *Roads to Success*, a syndicated television series profiling African American role models.) And Erving still has promotional contracts with the NBA, Coca-Cola USA, Converse, Hardees, and Advanced Golf

Technologies. He also serves as a consultant to a Jack Nicklaus company, Golden Bear Sports Management.

But it was his purchase of the Coca-Cola bottling plant that sent him on his entrepreneurial way. Throughout the 1970s and early 1980s, Bruce Llewellyn, a prominent African American businessman, had been trying to buy into the soft-drink bottling business. At the same time, the Reverend Jesse Jackson and Operation Push were protesting the lack of minority representation at Coke's corporate level. In 1982, a year before the Sixers won the NBA championship, Llewellyn and Erving had dinner together in Tuckahoe, New York.

"I thought I had a good shot at getting the Philadelphia franchise, and I told Julius that I thought his name could be of invaluable assistance to me," recalls Llewellyn, whom Erving refers to as his "business role model." "We bought in at about $60 million," Llewellyn says, "and Julius became a director and shareholder. It was the first time in the industry for a major minority-owned bottler. Now the franchise is probably worth about five times our initial investment."

Because Erving secured the Coke deal while still an active player, by 1985 the impact was felt throughout the athletic world. To a whole new generation of athletes, Erving became a role model – not for his on-court moves but for his board-room success. To this day, Magic Johnson, whose entrepreneurial aspirations are well known, frequently calls Erving to discuss deals and business protocol. "I've always picked Doc's brain, and he's always been there for me," says Johnson, whose goal is to own an NBA franchise someday. "He paved the way for athletes to be involved in business. The things he did with Coke set the stage for me to become a businessman." When the opportunity arose in 1988 for Johnson to invest in Pepsi, he jumped at it, going into partnership with Earl Graves, another prominent African American businessman, to become executive vice president and one-third owner of a Pepsi distribution and sales company in Maryland. Unlike Erving's deal with Coke, Johnson is not a bottler; he simply contracts to distribute Pepsi products. But the business parallels between the two former superstars have perpetuated their friendly on-court rivalry.

"We have a good-natured sort of competition going on," Erving says, smiling. "As a matter of fact, when I was at the All-Star Game this year, Magic was sitting right behind me. I turned around, and there he was, drinking a Minute Maid soda. I said, 'That's a Coke product, my man.' He just wasn't thinking."

Still, despite the groundbreaking success of Erving's Coke deal, Llewellyn, who professes great admiration and affection for him, gets frustrated at his protégé's inability to focus on any one business interest. (When asked about his influence on Erving, Llewellyn laughs and says, "I damn sure didn't teach him how to go out and waste all his time playing golf.") About once a month Erving meets with plant customers, and his input is heard occasionally on marketing. But Llewellyn would like to see him take a more active role.

"If you call Julius a businessman, I'd have to ask your definition of the term," Llewellyn says. "He's been a good marketing type of person, but he's not a nine-to-five businessman who hires and fires and negotiates contracts. I've told Julius that if he doesn't get himself involved in something in an in-depth, full-time way, well, where's he going to be? At some point, somebody is going to say, 'Who the hell is that?' With me, Julius has stock, an investment. With the companies he endorses, he has short-term contracts. In the long pull, I keep telling him his interests would be better served to stick with his investments and see to it that they grow."

As he sits in the offices of the Erving Group – a converted three-bedroom apartment at the Academy House on Locust Street – Erving says the diversity was all part of the plan.

"I developed this portfolio because I just didn't want to be consumed by any one thing anymore," he says, accompanying me through the reception area on my way out. A bronze sculpture of his arm and hand palming a basketball sits on the floor. "To be the best in the world at something, and for a time I was considered the best in the world – that has to be all and everything. For sixteen years I was Dr. J, and that took on a life of its own. I don't want to be just a Coca-Cola bottler twenty-four hours a day, be the guy coming down the street in red and white – 'The Coca-Cola Man.'"

He stops in front of a collection of Dr. J *Sport* magazine covers that grace the wall. "For the first time in my life, I'm a free agent," he says. "I can go where I'm needed and do what I need to do. There's nothing that I wish for that's not available to me."

IT IS ELEVEN O'CLOCK in the morning, and Julius Erving is at the Cherry Hill offices of Score Board, Inc., a sports memorabilia marketing firm that distributes autographed copies of Dr. J playing cards.

He will sit here for the next three hours, signing cards as a company representative monitors the process for authenticity. I ask if his hand gets tired.

"No, man, I'm on automatic pilot when I do this," he says.

The cards he is signing today are from the 1978 season. On the front of each one is an action photo of the Doctor at work, gliding through the air, while an inset head-and-shoulders photo shows off the old Afro.

Looking at him now – business suit, glasses, graying hair – it is hard to fathom what he once was and the impact he once had. In basketball circles today, it has become commonplace to hear harsh revisionism applied to Erving's career, especially in light of Michael Jordan. Indeed, the numbers are not comparable. Erving averaged 22 points, seven rebounds and nearly four assists per game as an NBA player; Jordan, 32.3, six, and six. But a statistical comparison misses the point; evaluating Erving in terms of points and rebounds is like judging Martin Luther King Jr. on the basis of his administrative skills. Erving changed the culture of basketball – Jordan would still be running the three-man weave if it weren't for him – and, as only a handful of athletes have done, influenced popular culture as well.

"Julius wearing the Afro was a major statement," says Nelson George, author of *Elevating the Game: Black Men and Basketball* and a noted chronicler of black culture. "I remember when he cut it. The Afro was over when Julius cut his. I always looked at that as a sort of acquiescence to the NBA and the mainstream."

But if Erving's change in hairstyle was a concession to mainstream forces, he made no such accommodations in his game. More than anyone – more than Connie Hawkins, more than Earl Monroe – Erving raised playground basketball to respectability. As the quintessential one-on-one player, Erving's game was antithetical to the below-the-rim version taught at the local CYOs and by the Bobby Knights of the world. Throughout his eleven years with the Sixers, I can't recall Erving ever setting or using a screen; instead, his four teammates would go to one side of the floor to "isolate" Julius on his man while the Spectrum crowd collectively held its breath. Though his outside shot was streaky at best, it didn't matter: He could take anybody.

Turn on any college or pro game today and you can see his legacy. Dunking – once the shot of choice for "hot-dog" or undisciplined players – has become fundamental to the game. They call Atlanta's Dominique Wilkins the Human Highlight Film, but Erving invented the highlight.

Predictably, when he entered the league in 1976, Erving's game didn't sit well with the staid NBA establishment. Celtic "genius" Red Auerbach said, "Julius Erving is a nice kid, but he's not a great player." When the Sixers played the Portland Trailblazers in the finals that season, it was a series rife with racial overtones – white suburban basketball versus the black street game. The Trailblazers, relying on intricate screening and backdoor cutting, won. (At the time, basketball aficionados read too much into the Trailblazers' victory; the 76ers probably would have won the series had George McGinnis not joined the Bricklayers Union for five of the six games.) The questions back then about how his game would fare in the NBA still rankle Erving today.

"It was just a simple bias," he says. "It was annoying to hear these critiques about black ballplayers. People would say, 'This player has all this natural ability, but driving in there and jumping over somebody for a dunk isn't a smart play. The smart play is to make three or four passes and get a lay-up.' Well, it's a smart play when you get your desired result, you know? Black players would get stereotyped as just having natural ability, but I knew that when I first started playing ball, I couldn't play a lick."

For those first couple years in Philly, Dr. J truly was the Brother from Another Planet. With the Afro and goatee he looked like a Black Panther, and his street game was just as radical. But his demeanor was not at all consistent with the image, and his nonthreatening, dignified style off the court endeared him to Philly fans and, ultimately, to basketball fans worldwide.

"Yeah my game was contrary to my personality," he says now. "My game was red, and I'm blue. My game was revolutionary, and I'm a very controlled person. I had to deal with that a lot, because socially, after a game, I would just want to get some dinner, go home, and go to bed. But people would be, like, 'Yo, Dr. J is here, he's the life of the party.' And I'd be, like, 'You ain't talking about me.'"

Still, the love affair he had with the fans of his city is a testament to his innate ability to, in his words, "cross over." Coming of age in the seventies, Erving was part of an era that saw black culture – specifically music, with the ascendancy of Motown and artists like Stevie Wonder and Michael Jackson – woo white consumers. A product of his generation, he felt obligated to do the same in his industry. He embraced his role as a symbol of the possibilities of integration, a representative of upwardly mobile black America.

"In the late seventies, there was tremendous racial separation in Philadelphia, with the whole MOVE situation and Mayor Rizzo and the strong-arm tactics of that era," Erving says as he watches himself slowly twist the NBA Championship ring he wears on his right hand. "People were just reluctant to leave their neighborhoods. The Fishtowners stayed in Fishtown, Germantowners in Germantown, South Philadelphians in South Philly. You could see the city composed of different pockets of self-interest, and no one was looking out for the whole. I saw this, and my goal was to move about with freedom and respect in all the different communities. 'Crossover' became an important term for me, because it wasn't a black thing anymore. All of a sudden, you had white adults telling their kids to grow up and be like Julius Erving. And it all culminated in the parade of 1983, when we won the championship. I remember coming down Broad Street and seeing all these different people and it was, like, 'Wait a minute – they ain't all from this neighborhood. A lot of these people crossed the line to celebrate together.'"

Ten years later, a new generation had forsaken the crossover tradition, as illustrated by Charles Barkley's in-your-face public persona. The hip-hop generation is not as interested in making accommodations to white taste. In the winter of 1992, Barkley and Spike Lee's interview in *The Source*, a hip-hop journal, was titled "Nineties Niggers." In May 1993's *Playboy*, Barkley talks about the fans wanting black athletes to "know their places." And in 1992, Craig Hodges, then with the Chicago Bulls, excoriated Michael Jordan and other top black athletes for not speaking out politically. (Over the course of two days, I grilled Erving to no avail on his politics; "I've always had political convictions," he says, "but my business interests handicap me" from discussing them publicly.)

Yet even Jordan, despite his crossover commercial appeal, does things that Erving never would have attempted. He wears the X hats that have become the symbol of the hip-hop generation, hangs out with Spike Lee, and even "dissed" George Bush by not showing up when the Bulls were invited to the White House after winning their first title. In light of the generational surge away from Erving's vision of integration, it would be easy to criticize him for so smoothly moving into the white establishment – easy but shortsighted.

"This current generation doesn't know much about Dr. J other than that he's a very revered figure who had a cool nickname," says Nelson George. "But Julius employs African

Americans and underwrites minority scholarships without shouting about it. My impression is that he believes in doing."

And Erving's sociopolitical influence transcended even his own intentions. Throughout the seventies, Julius Erving was a walking racial discussion even when he was reluctant to speak about the issue; his game itself was the message. In his book *Elevating the Game*, Nelson George discusses the black aesthetic that came to characterize basketball, a style that Dr. J had the largest hand in creating. In the mid-eighties, I used to watch the playground ball at 145th Street and Malcolm X Boulevard in Harlem, keeping a careful distance from the courts to avoid any temptations to embarrass myself. But what I saw, time and again, was the imprint left by Erving. I saw guys who cared about showmanship, who celebrated shots based on their degree of difficulty rather than just their results. The quality of their moves always took priority over the score, and the real competition was over who could exhibit the most creativity; it was basketball as art form, a manifestation of the black aesthetic that is Dr. J's legacy.

And, just as important, the joyousness of the playground was infectious and in sharp contrast to the repressed nature of the suburban game many of us grew up playing. It was black athletes who started the celebratory traditions of the high five and the end-zone spike, as well as the current in-your-face craze of trash talking. But even though his energetic and passionate playground game spawned such posturing, Erving disdains these modern manifestations.

"In the seventies, you were supposed to ignore the cameras," he says. "Now, guys play to the cameras. You've got Michael Jordan shooting foul shots with his eyes closed—that's calling attention to yourself. My game might have spawned the creation of the highlight, but that was for the fan to celebrate, not the player. What's to celebrate? To me, you celebrate when you surprise yourself. Dunking on people for me was the rule, rather than the exception. Before a game, I always knew I'd be dunking on somebody. I didn't have to talk trash or do any of that stuff. We're living in a time of instant gratification, and these kids today want to capture the thrill of the moment."

I tell Dr. J I'm a little surprised how much he sounds like those members of the establishment who couldn't understand his game twenty years ago.

Julius Erving looks up from the cards he's been signing and thinks for a moment. "Maybe it is a bit of a contradiction," he says.

He returns his attention to the pile of cards in front of him. He has an hour to go, and he is on automatic pilot.

IT IS GETTING LATE, and Julius Erving and I are sitting in his office. I tell him that despite his fame, my sense is that people still wonder what he's like.

He pauses, no doubt contemplating just how much of himself he wishes to reveal. He says that when you've done things "larger than life," it becomes hard for people to relate to you. He takes a drink from his Coke, still debating whether to say more. "Really, I'm just a guy," he says. "You cut me, and I'm gonna bleed."

Before I leave, I take out my wallet. For close to a decade I've carried around a folded-up black-and-white magazine photo of Dr. J, taken during a 1978 game against the Knicks at Madison Square Garden. He is flying through the air, higher than I've ever seen Jordan jump, eyes even with the rim, dunking over 6'8" Lonnie Shelton while Bob McAdoo runs for cover. For Erving, it is probably just one of a million dunks. I ask him if he recognizes the guy soaring in the photo.

"Oh, my God," he says slowly, leaning forward, eyes locked on the picture. The years begin to melt away, as does his cool veneer. "I'm looking at the rim. I must have been scared, I'm up so high. I remember this play."

The phone is ringing, and Erving stands. I think he's about to answer it, but he doesn't seem to hear anything.

"I remember, after I dunked this ball, it rattled around the rim, and I had to put my hand on the backboard like this to keep from crashing into it," he says, standing in the middle of his office, pirouetting, acting out this fifteen-year-old memory. I wonder if anyone down on Locust Street happens to be looking up at this image of Dr. J high in the sky, reenacting an old flight pattern. "I landed flat on my feet, like this. They called a blocking foul on Shelton."

Ray Wilson, Erving's business manager and longtime confidant, has answered the phone in the outer office and pokes his head in. "Turk wants to know when you'll be leaving," he says, referring to Julius's wife, Turquoise.

Erving doesn't hear. "Look at McAdoo," he says, laughing, still transfixed by the photo. "He's, like, 'You take him!'"

"Julius, Turk wants to know when you're heading home," Wilson repeats.

Erving says nothing.

"Julius?" Wilson says again.

"Just loading up my briefcase, Ray," he says, never taking his eyes from the photo. Then he lets out a low whistle and hands the picture back to me. It's time for Julius Erving, middle-aged businessman, to make his nightly commute to the suburbs.

10

Magic Johnson
Builds an Empire

AROUND THE TIME his teammate Kareem Abdul-Jabbar declared bankruptcy in the mid-eighties, the Los Angeles Lakers star Earvin (Magic) Johnson found himself in-bounding the ball during a game right in front of Joe Smith of Elektra-Asylum Records and Peter Guber of Sony Pictures, Lakers courtside season-ticket holders. Johnson had always been aware of the fates of black athletes past – the fortunes lost by the likes of Jesse Owens, Joe Louis, Muhammad Ali. And so, before passing the ball to a teammate, Johnson turned to the pair and asked, "How do I get into business?"

The two knew that the basketball star needed a guiding hand, and within days, they arranged a meeting for Johnson with Hollywood *über*-agent Mike Ovitz. But Johnson, so used to electrifying crowds every night on the court, couldn't get Ovitz to crack a smile. "I don't do business with athletes," Ovitz said; Johnson *heard*, "I don't do business with dumb jocks," a stereotype Johnson had long battled. When Ovitz abruptly got up to leave, saying, "Someone will show you out," the 6'9" Johnson – suddenly, stunningly alone in the conference room – felt a foot shorter for the first time in his life.

When Ovitz's office summoned Johnson for a return engagement three weeks later, Johnson knew his macho locker-room brethren would have advised him to stay away. But Johnson already aspired to be unlike other athletes. "You gotta take your ego out of this," he counseled himself, in keeping with his selfless style of play. Once the player was there, Ovitz – who had done some checking into Johnson's background since their last go-round – agreed to be a mentor. But first he slammed a stack of publications on the conference table: the *Wall Street Journal, Business Week, Fortune.* "It's time you got your head out of the sports pages," he told his new and eager protégé.

MORE THAN a decade later, Johnson, now forty-one, stands in his bustling strip mall in the heart of South Central Los Angeles. Within this complex is his Starbucks and his T.G.I. Friday's, and it's only four miles to his state-of-the art fifteen-plex movie theater.

A parade of evening shoppers stop to hug or high-five Johnson, who is wearing a Fubu jersey and jean shorts. By day, he is Mr. Johnson to his staff in the Beverly Hills office where he oversees a business empire that includes more than $500 million of property in heretofore depressed inner-city areas. But here, where he can be found three or four nights a week, he is Magic, the former basketball player, a charismatic figure who keeps coming around so his customers know he's not just another athlete selling his name and likeness to white businesspeople. But he is also here thanks to an insatiable need for attention: One friend observes that he's addicted to the spotlight, and Johnson himself admits that he feeds off the love he's shown here. It's as though he has found a way to extend the cheers of his playing days.

Some of those flocking to him offer thanks for rejuvenating a moribund neighborhood that others have failed to resuscitate in the years since the Los Angeles riots ravaged these very streets. As Johnson heads toward Starbucks, a baggy-pantsed, backward-capped, morose-looking teenager on a cell phone passes by; glancing up, he does a double take. "Magic Johnson!" he cries, handing the phone toward the former player. "Say hi to my grandma!" Johnson stops, his smile widening. "Hello, Grandma," he says while the kid bounces on the balls of his feet, the scowl morphing into a grin. "Your grandson was thinking of you – the first thing he said was 'Say hi to my grandma.' So he presents himself well, which means you've done your job, Grandma. Who raised him?" Johnson looks at the kid. "Well you and moms done your job, Grandma. I love you too, Grandma. Okay, here he is."

Inside Starbucks, Johnson's gleaming face adorns one wall, and HIV and AIDS brochures are at the counter. "See, people say all kinds of things about black people, but look at this," Johnson says, motioning toward the packed tables. At one, a young man works on a laptop. At another, a couple of college students pore over a stack of open textbooks. On the patio, fathers are schooling their sons in chess. Johnson moves toward them, smiling, hugging his own upper torso. "Man, I want to cry every time I see that," he says, before stage-whispering, *"Because they never had this before here."*

Johnson employs roughly three thousand people who live in inner-city neighborhoods across the country. Over the next two hours, as Johnson sips herbal tea and tirelessly plays host, he talks about the satisfaction of employing people. His recent venture in Harlem, where his multiplex opened in July 2000 as part of the Harlem USA mall, has sparked a renaissance of 125th Street. Last summer, after the

Harlem theater hired one hundred people from the five thousand who had waited in line to apply, Johnson decided he wanted his new staff to go through four weeks of rigorous training. On opening day, dozens of young men and women stood before him in pressed uniforms. "Just looking at those faces, the hope and pride," he says, remembering the scene, "that may have been the best moment of my life, right there."

Later, outside, as he ambles toward his black Bentley convertible, an elderly woman has him sign a paper bag that she says she'll cherish forever. "We need a bookstore next, Magic," she pleads, and the exchange is reminiscent of the genesis of his partnership with T.G.I. Friday's. That deal was hatched in 1999 after a seventy-something woman in Atlanta told him she'd never been able to get a salad in her neighborhood.

He gets in the car. "A bookstore," he says softly. "Okay. We're going to look into that now."

THOUGH MICHAEL JORDAN is celebrated for his boardroom moves, he accumulated his wealth mostly by selling his name. Johnson, by contrast, is an entrepreneur with Rockefeller-like ambitions who says he wants to do things no black man has ever done. He is becoming a post–civil-rights era role model for hip-hop jocks who reject the Jordan example and see Johnson as the walking embodiment of Malcolm X's dream – he is a black-run, inner-city business unto himself. And he predicts he'll go public in the next five years. In addition to his theaters in Los Angeles and Harlem, there are others in Atlanta, Houston, and Cleveland, and more on the way. All rank among the nation's top fifty theaters in gross sales.

In 2000, Johnson took part in a joint venture with Starbucks to create more than twenty Starbucks shops. All per-

form in the top five in their respective regions; the South
Central store, for example, where lines snake out the door on
weekend nights, is among the most profitable of Los Angeles's four hundred–odd stores. In addition, Johnson has
started a music label, in conjunction with MCA, and a pro-
motional arm that staged the recent Dr. Dre and Eminem
tour and that is readying Prince for the road. There are plans
for six T.G.I. Friday's and a string of Magic Clubs – twenty-
four-hour inner-city fitness facilities. He also created a foundation that has raised more than $15 million for HIV and
AIDS awareness since 1991, and that each year sends roughly
forty disadvantaged high school students to college for four
years.

A self-described "control freak," Johnson is up every
weekday morning at 6:30. First he downs a twice-daily pro-
tease-inhibitor "cocktail" – though there is no trace of HIV in
his blood, the virus lies dormant somewhere in his body –
and then he calls back East for the previous day's box office
receipts. Every Monday, just before eating a salad for lunch
at his desk in his sparse, meticulously organized office, he
holds a conference call with his theater managers and
Loews representatives, during which he decides precisely
how many screens will show each film.

Johnson has always harbored a business fantasy. His
work ethic came from Earvin Sr., who by night worked as a
spot welder in the General Motors plant; days, he collected
garbage, often taking his son along on his route. So it was no
surprise when Earvin Jr. approached Joel Ferguson and
Gregory Eaton, two area African American businessmen
who drove Mercedes Benzes. Johnson not only asked for a
job but told them he was going to be just like them someday.
They hired him to clean their offices each weekend, but what
they didn't know was that he'd spend a good part of his time

sitting at their desks, fantasizing, hitting the intercom, conducting mock meetings, kicking his feet up. From there, he'd hit the public basketball courts, where he'd pretend to be taking the last shot of the seventh game of the NBA Finals, over and over again.

Even when his hoop dream came true, Johnson still yearned to be a businessman. When he hooked up with Ovitz, who walked him through his first business deal with Pepsi-Cola in 1988, Johnson's career was set in motion. "We had a meeting with the president of Pepsi," says Ovitz. "And Earvin insisted on rehearsing before the meeting. We threw questions at him and he fielded them. When it came to the real meeting, he knocked their doors off." The arrangement with Pepsi, 25 percent ownership of a Maryland distribution plant, marked Johnson's first foray into ownership.

In the early nineties, Johnson teamed up with Ken Lombard, an African American investment banker who is the president of Magic Johnson Development. Lombard secured a $50 million commitment from California's largest pension fund for the purchase of three inner-city shopping centers. Soon after, when Johnson approached Loews Cineplex Entertainment with the idea of an inner-city multiplex – conveniently situated near his shopping outlets – he was armed with research from Lombard. Twenty-five percent of all moviegoers are African Americans, Johnson pointed out to Lawrence Ruisi, the Loews CEO; yet there are hardly any theaters in African American neighborhoods. Ruisi was sold, especially when Johnson and Lombard explained that rental rates per square foot would be roughly $13, compared with close to $30 in the suburbs; moreover, Johnson argued that even in bad economic times, "black people have always gone to the movies as a way to escape."

On opening weekend, Johnson fretted that there wouldn't be enough hot dogs at the theater's concession stand. The Loews concessionaire told him not to worry. Sure enough, the hot dogs sold out by midnight on Friday.

"See, you've got to understand black people," Johnson says today. "I know my customer base, because I'm it. I told Loews, black people are going to eat dinner at the movies – those hot dogs are our dinner. Same with the drinks. Our soda sales were just okay. I said black people love flavored drinks, because we were raised on Kool-Aid. So we put in punch and strawberry soda and orange, and the numbers went through the roof."

Though the theater industry is struggling – four chains have filed for bankruptcy, and even Johnson's fifty-fifty partner Loews is laboring – Johnson's theaters are flourishing; by the end of 2000, they served their 10 millionth customer. In part that's because they have become de facto community centers, where visitors can get their blood pressure checked and parents can periodically get free immunization shots for their kids. Teenagers are welcome to hang out in the lobby and play video games, even if they're not seeing a film – as long as they don't wear gang colors.

It's this sense of community that sold Howard Schultz, the chairman of Starbucks. Schultz had never taken on a partner before, but he agreed to convene with Johnson and Lombard because, as a longtime basketball fan, he couldn't pass up the chance to meet Magic. "It became clear," Schultz recalls about that first meeting, "that no one knows more about African American spending power than Earvin. I was expecting a basketball player, but here was this businessman telling me there are 40 million African Americans who spent over $500 billion last year."

Schultz agreed to visit the South Central theaters on a Friday night. "At Starbucks," he says, "we talk about our stores being a third place for our customers between work and home, and I realized that's what Earvin had done. He built a sense of community. I saw graffiti everywhere in South Central – except on his building."

Johnson told Schultz that his people hungered for meeting places. "If we build it, they'll come," Johnson pledged. Over the objections of many within his company, Schultz agreed to a fifty-fifty partnership with Johnson on seven stores – a limited agreement that was expanded once the spectacular numbers started coming in.

Starbucks is fiercely protective of its brand, so Johnson had to persuade Schultz to tailor Starbucks' product to the inner city. As a result, there is a fast-selling sweet-potato pie and peach cobbler on the menu. And since each Starbucks comes with custom-made CD players that play only tunes compiled by the company's music department in Seattle, Johnson lobbied for a collection of African American music. Now visitors to Johnson's Starbucks shops hear Stevie Wonder or Miles Davis in the background, not James Taylor. (There is no rap music – Johnson knows it's not palatable to all generations.) When expanding overseas, Johnson points out, companies don't think twice about strategic partnerships with local experts who can navigate the cultural terrain. But chains haven't done the same in urban communities.

That may be changing. After it was announced that Johnson's theaters and a Starbucks were coming to Harlem, other stores followed: HMV, Disney, Old Navy, Modell's Sporting Goods. It raises some vexing questions for Johnson. For all his egalitarian talk, his strategy pushes corporate commercialism, and it hasn't jump-started an empowerment trend either. Instead, he has enriched the bottom lines of traditionally white companies and so far has been little more than the lead blocker for white-owned chains, easing their expansion into urban areas. So he recently talked to Puffy Combs about opening an uptown restaurant, and to the hip-hop impresario Russell Simmons about bringing Simmons's retail clothing store to Harlem. "Now white Americans are buying up Harlem brownstones," Johnson laments. "Black people have been conditioned to live for today. I'm helping to rebuild Harlem, but we as a people won't own it."

MAGIC JOHNSON is about to do something few businesspeople and even fewer athletes do: endorse a candidate for public office. In the lobby of his theaters, he stands before TV cameras in September 2000 next to Jim Hahn, the Los Angeles city attorney and Democratic candidate for mayor. Hahn is the winner of the Magic Sweepstakes; for months now, candidates vying to succeed Mayor Richard Riordan have lobbied for Johnson's imprimatur, including a couple of Latino politicians. Johnson settled on Hahn, who is white, in part because Hahn grew up in South Central.

"Jim Hahn understands," Johnson says, while the cameras seem to struggle with the challenge of fitting both Johnson and the comparatively diminutive Hahn in their frames. "Most of the candidates haven't even been to Crenshaw. But this is a man who grew up here and who cares."

It's a striking moment, not so much for what he says but for the fact that he's saying anything at all. Thirty years ago, it was not uncommon for black athletes, led by Ali, Jim Brown, and the Olympic sprinters John Carlos and Tommy Smith, to wade into politics. But as athletes have risen to the pinnacle of commodity culture, they have been less willing to speak out. Asked a few years back why he didn't endorse Harvey Gantt, a credible black challenger to Senator Jesse Helms in his home state of North Carolina, Michael Jordan replied, "Republicans buy Nikes too."

Johnson's smile may engender Jordan-like "crossover" appeal, but his warmth masks a more radical agenda that dovetails with his business interests—unlike Jordan, he is not selling anything to suburban Republicans. So Johnson plays to the cameras and endorses a white candidate, all the while embracing Dr. Dre and the corn-rowed, tattooed, gangsta-rapping Philadelphia 76ers star Allen Iverson. Yet Johnson's support of hip-hoppers makes ideological sense, given that they revolutionized the music business by insisting on owning their master recordings, something that crossover artists like Marvin Gaye and Stevie Wonder never did. And like the rappers, Johnson doesn't mince words for fear of offending white sensibilities. At a panel discussion at the University of Southern California during the Democratic National Convention, Johnson said of the Republicans, "They didn't want us before; they don't want us now." And about the Democrats he said, "People, we've got to make sure Gore follows our plan—the black plan."

For Johnson, the black plan is about ownership. "Black people, we don't own nothing," he said at USC. "They'll let us entertain them. We have always been the best at that. But we don't own teams, we don't own record companies, we don't own movie studios. Now I employ three thousand black people"—many in the crowd started cheering—"I'm not saying that for applause. There are about five thousand black athletes in all of sports. If you multiply that by three thousand, where are we at? *One-point-five million employed black peo-*

ple." Johnson is trying to spread that empowerment gospel to a generation of athletes who have come to see themselves not only as entertainers but as entrepreneurs as well. "When I first met Magic," recalls Shaquille O'Neal, "he said, 'Getting your name in the paper is fun, but you've got to own things and employ our people instead of just taking money.' That's stuck with me."

O'Neal has become a businessman in his own right, choosing Compton as the location for his record label, T.W.IsM. ("The World Is Mine"). Every week, athletes ranging from the football star Bruce Smith to the basketball player Patrick Ewing seek Johnson's business advice. Iverson sought Johnson's counsel a couple of years back, when he decided to jettison his agent, David Falk, the man who first brought Nike and Jordan together in the eighties. Iverson and other young players, Johnson says, often ask him how he made the transition from court to boardroom. "I tell them I showed up on time to every meeting. I didn't come in wearing all the jewelry and I surrounded myself with people like Ken Lombard who were smarter than me."

THE ROOTS of Johnson's economic populism can be traced to the moment in 1991 when he announced that he was HIV-positive. He remembers puttering around the house in the days that followed, aware of the silent phone, supported only by members of the South Central church that he and his wife, Cookie, attended. "After the whole myth of being an athlete stops, the only people left are the people in the community," he says. And he remembers the companies, such as Nestle, that rushed to sever ties with him.

"When you are playing ball, there's a tendency to be politically correct, to not do or say anything that'll turn off endorsers," Johnson says later in his trailer, a couple of hours before a star-studded fashion show in front of forty-five hundred kids to benefit HIV and AIDS research. Though he explains that, deep down, he always wanted to take stands on issues important to black America, it wasn't until his experience with HIV, when he realized he had nothing left to lose, that he was spurred into action. In 1992, he not only resigned in protest from President George Bush's AIDS commission, he also publicly blasted Bush for fighting the disease with "lip service and photo opportunities."

On the fashion show's runway, Johnson models a leopard-skin overcoat, basking in the attention of a rapt crowd. Then he watches the show enthusiastically, cupping his hands to his mouth and yelling, "This is old school!" when a Motown tune comes on, languidly grooving his shoulders to the beat. His smile is his unique brand, and it is more iconic even than Jordan's Nike-devised leaping silhouette. The smile sells both him and what he's selling, be it a money-making venture or a tough-minded prescription for African American empowerment. It was there that day when the doctors told him that a sense of optimism would be key to battling HIV: "You mean I can beat this by being positive?" he said. "It's over, then. I've won." And it's there now, as Johnson explains that, though how he got his disease was not heroic, he decided to deal with it heroically. And it remains on his face when he gives voice to his latest mission.

"Now I've got to teach these young brothers that you don't have to sell out to do good," he says. "I tell those guys all the time, You don't realize how much power you've got. Use it in your community. You can make money *and* keep it real back home and lift all of us up."

11

The Business of Rebellion

IN 1996, A LANKY seventeen-year-old basketball player in St. Louis saw something about himself on the tag to a pair of shorts. The image was of a faceless, raceless, brawny ballplayer in mid-move. "That's me," the kid thought. "A ballplayer." Tag in hand, he found a tattoo parlor and had the caricature etched into the skin of his upper arm, with the words "The Law" above it (because when he's playing defense, he's got you on lockdown) and "Silky Smooth" underneath.

"I was looking for something that said, 'Playing ball is what I'm about,' you know what I'm saying?" the kid, Larry Hughes, recalls. By 1999, Hughes played for the Philadelphia 76ers of the National Basketball Association and was paid six figures to endorse the brand that he so closely identified with three years earlier – And 1, an upstart apparel and footwork company that is carving out a niche as the street-level alternative to mighty Nike. But back then, Hughes was just a young guy who fell in love with these quirky trash-talking T-shirts – "Call 911, I'm on Fire" – and this logo, the Player, that somehow captured the macho attitude of the street game.

"You don't have to talk a lot of junk on the playground when you got the Player on your arm and you're wearing an

And 1 shirt," says Hughes, whose soft-spoken persona seems to morph into a lifelike, snarling replica of his cartoon alter ego when he steps on court. "I used to make a move, score on my man and just stare at him while pointing to the tattoo. Like, 'This is what you just got.' That gets into guys' heads."

Hughes isn't the only one taken with And 1 and the Player. DePaul University's Quentin Richardson, one of the best college players in the country in 1999, has a tattoo much like Hughes's. At the 1998 Adidas ABCD camp, a gathering of the nation's top one hundred high school players, four kids had the tattoo. Like countless others, they had opted for a logo devised six years before by three white basketball junkies in their twenties who bypassed dreary careers on Wall Street to start a basketball clothing company. They thought they'd be in business for a year.

SETH BERGER, the thirty-one-year-old CEO of And 1, a native New Yorker who played pickup ball throughout the city – including one summer at the famed Rucker Tournament – realized in 1993 that basketball lacked a company that reflected the culture of its bedrock customers. So he devised a marketing strategy that favors outlaws and playground legends over sanitized NBA starters, as well as rap-promotion techniques over corporate advertising.

And 1 built slowly, finally bursting into the national consciousness in the spring of 1999 with the Latrell Sprewell "American Dream" TV commercials. Sprewell is the cornrowed forward who was suspended for choking his coach and then returned to lead the Knicks to the NBA finals in June 1999. By then he had supplanted Mike Tyson and Dennis Rodman as sports' preeminent anti-hero. "People say I'm America's worst nightmare," Sprewell says defiantly in the ad, while piercing electric guitar notes mimic Jimi Hendrix's version of "The Star-Spangled Banner." "I say I'm the American Dream."

And 1's aggressive, youthful image offended the sports mainstream, but it certainly didn't hurt it with its target audience. Suddenly, a little-known company seemingly was everywhere, and sales took off.

The privately held company, which by 1999 had seventy-one employees at its suburban Philadelphia headquarters, projects gross sales for 2000 of $120 million and claims to have already secured the number-two spot to Nike in basketball apparel sales. (Not that And 1 is an imminent threat to Nike's overall dominance: With gross sales in the $9 billion range, Nike still controls some 25 percent of the athletic-wear market.) And 1's performance is all the more remarkable for coming at a time when sneaker sales overall have slumped, as brown boots like Timberlands have become more fashionable. But Berger doesn't care what kids wear when they're at a party. He cares only what's on their feet and their backs on the basketball court.

And that's why the playground bad-boy image is so important. There's no real difference between, say, a pair of droopy shorts from Nike and a pair of droopy shorts from And 1. Berger and his partners recognize that the key to And 1's future – and to challenging Nike, the goal of their current five-year plan – is in expanding while staying true to its street roots.

"We have to do things other brands aren't willing to do, like signing Sprewell," says Jay Gilbert, thirty, Berger's partner and the company's director of product and marketing. "And the most important thing we have to guard against is becoming corporate. We've got to keep reinventing this thing."

Like the hip-hop culture to which it is intimately linked, And 1 is in the business of rebellion. The upstart company certainly did not invent the hip-hop–hoops connection: Basketball players such as Shaquille O'Neal, Chris Webber, and Kobe Bryant have become rappers, and rappers such as Master P (who recently tried to make it in the NBA with the Toronto Raptors) and Mase have long been known as "ballers" on inner-city playgrounds. But And 1 is the first athletic-wear company to capitalize so thoroughly on hip-hip's most rebellious aspects.

Rap and basketball share a youthful machismo and aggressiveness that is reflected in the And 1 trash-talking tees and the scowl of the Player logo. And at the street level, both are informed by an anti-corporate, anti-establishment streak, as evidenced not only by the ascendance of And 1 but by the rise of fashion labels FUBU ("For Us, By Us"), Mecca, and Ecko. All are companies that have succeeded because they have come up from the street without a corporate identity, lending them a hip, word-of-mouth cachet.

Last spring, And 1 hooked up with Set Free, a recording artist and producer from Tommy Boy Records who knew that hip-hop labels had long created demand by sending out "street teams" to hype CDs before their official release. So And 1 produced the *And 1 Mix Tape*: a compilation of video clips of playground legends named Skip to My Lou, Headache, and Half-Man, Half-Amazing doing what they do best at Rucker Park and other inner-city basketball meccas, to a soundtrack of as-yet-unreleased hip-hop tracks courtesy of artists such as Prince Paul, Redman, and the Wu Tang Clan.

Free promoted the And 1 tape like a rap single, turning it overnight into a playground status symbol. When, months later, And 1 gave the tape to Dr. Jay's, a New York–based sporting-goods chain, to use as a "gift with purchase," nearly 450 items of And 1 merchandise moved in one weekend in one store alone. The *Mix Tape* made its debut in October 1999 at Footaction stores nationwide, even as street teams began to promote volume 2.

The tape was such a success, in fact, that And 1 went out and hired six New York City playground legends as official endorsers of the brand. The company is paying them thousands of dollars each (more than some NBA players get for sneaker endorsements these days) and sending them on the road – a hip-hop Harlem Globetrotters, if you will, complete with courtside DJs.

But Berger's boldest move has been the Sprewell ad, which illustrates the seismic shift at work in the NBA and pop culture at large: the ascendancy of a generation of hip-hop jocks who are viewed as "real" in youth culture because of their seeming lack of interest in placating white taste.

For decades, black athletes have been made over for the comfort of white America; Madison Avenue may have marketed Joe Namath, John McEnroe, and Andre Agassi as rebels in the tradition of James Dean, but only nonthreatening black athletes saw any real endorsement opportunities. Commercial opportunities were denied to those who wouldn't conform to advertisers' ideas of what a "safe" black athlete should be – like Muhammad Ali in his prime or Tommy Smith and John Carlos, the Olympic sprinters who in 1968 raised black-gloved fists in a symbol of Black Power. Even Charles Barkley, the odd Nike ad notwithstanding, once claimed he lost out on some $10 million a year because of his unwillingness to "say what the media wants me to say."

But now And 1 is able to tap a vibrant, cross-cultural youth market eager to embrace sports stars spouting anti-establishment mores. So the sneakers of bland, supposed Jordan heirs such as Grant Hill and Kobe Bryant haven't sold nearly as well as those promoted by players with more exciting and dangerous images, such as Allen Iverson and Sprewell.

In the aftermath of the Sprewell ad, Berger heard himself derided as a white guy who is exploiting black culture for profit. In response, he says, half in jest, that of the company's six equity partners, "two are black, two are Jewish and two are just plain white." Even more significant, he argues, playing to urban culture is not the same as playing to a strictly black clientele. You can be hip-hop, in other words, and not be black. "MTV helped create a youth culture that sees beyond race," Berger says, noting that his products – like rap music itself – sell to suburban whites as well as to inner-city blacks. "As long as you're authentic. And And 1 is about ball."

INSIDE THE suburban setting of And 1's offices, the mood is all playground, all the time. Key positions are held by black and white ballplayers fresh out of college, who negotiate deals with retailers and licensees while wearing baggy shorts and caps on backward. At lunchtime, groups of them play full-court hoops; in fact, the And 1 job interview process includes applicants showing how much game they've got. Even the secretaries pepper their speech with hoopspeak: "My bad," they'll say when a call gets lost.

It is going on seven years since Berger first came up with the idea of And 1. Researching a paper while getting his MBA from the Wharton School at the University of Pennsylvania, he found that there were 45 million frequent and casual basketball players nationwide. "These people need cool stuff," he would tell his professors.

It began with the shirts. In those days, Berger, Gilbert, and Tommy Austin, the third founder, all spent nights on the floor of their original office-apartment. By day, they'd storm into sporting-goods stores, hawking T-shirts. Gradually, they caught on. In year three, the partners met with the NBA star Larry Johnson to try to persuade him to wear the shirts. When the meeting degenerated into Gilbert and Berger trash-talking about each other's games, Johnson broke into a wide, gold-toothed smile. "I see," he said. "You just some young guys looking to take care of business." Though he's no longer wearing And 1, Johnson put the company on the map, as did a later, brief shoe deal with Stephon Marbury, now with the Phoenix Suns.

The playground jocularity that so impressed Johnson is still on display. Some of And 1's best trash-talk T-shirt slogans – "I drive by you so much I should pay a toll" or "I'm the bus driver, I take everybody to school" – come straight from their own boisterous pickup games every day at lunch. The partners built the brand by acting as their own focus group and doing market research themselves, right in the playground. Berger knew the Coordinator sneaker was going to be a hit when one kid in a schoolyard wanted to buy it then and there, even though he had only one sample sneaker.

The partners still play ball, but they don't get out to many urban playgrounds anymore. They've left their twenties; they have wives and children and live in the suburbs. So they've made a pact to give up decision-making powers to their young hires. It was those kids who pushed for Sprewell's "American Dream" commercial. "The kids were right," Berger says. "To a high school ballplayer, Sprewell is the American Dream – a self-made NBA all-star. And if you're comfortable with a different style, a different fashion, then you totally respect what someone like Spree is all about."

Similarly, it was Phin Barnes, director of footwear design, and Dave Lewis, director of advertising, both twenty-four, who came up with the idea for the *Mix Tape* – and to release it underground, unadulterated, so it looks like a bootlegged copy. Volume 1 features the Globetrotter-like showmanship of Skip to My Lou, whose real name is Rafer Alston and who rides the bench of the NBA's Milwaukee Bucks. It's breathtaking footage, but Gilbert had it on his shelf, using it to impress his friends without a thought to its business potential. "And then the young guys smacked me on the head and told me I was sitting on a gold mine and that I'm old and soft," he recounts, laughing. "We get pretty competitive around here, so I was like, 'To heck with you, I'm not soft.' And the *Mix Tape* was born."

THE PLAYGROUND LEGEND is a staple of basketball's history. Countless stories through the years have documented the can't-miss schoolyard talents who have fallen prey to drugs, bad grades, or an unwillingness to temper their improvisational styles. For every Sprewell and Iverson there are guys like Half Man–Half Amazing, Main Event, Future, and Headache, for whom fans at the 155th Street park throw Tylenol onto the court when he dribbles through the legs of his defender. These are the And 1 All-Stars, guys who would be in the NBA were it not for their personal "if only" narratives.

"You don't understand, my NBA is the Rucker," says Future, whose real name is Malloy Nesmith. Future and his pals like to talk about the day in the summer of 1999 when he scored forty-two points on the Milwaukee Bucks' Ray Allen at 155th Street. Now Future is joined by his teammates at a midtown Planet Hollywood, where their passion for the game knows no moment of silence. They talk over one another, barking out stories, talking trash about NBA players like Allen who have dared to invade their turf. "You come in my house—" Future says.

"You better bring you're 'A' game or you be Jerry Stackhouse!" chimes in Headache, referring to another NBA star who, they say, had a rough night with these guys. For three hours, they exchange high-fives, reenact old dunks and crossovers, express amazement that Chris Childs (since moved to the Toronto Raptors) and Charlie Ward are the point guards on their beloved Knicks and they're not, and hope that the And 1 tour will lead to NBA riches.

For years, they say, major companies have come to 155th Street to use them. They've done photo shoots, videos, commercials. And, if they were lucky, the players were allowed to keep the gear they were asked to wear for the event. "When And 1 came to us, it was, like, the first time anyone said, 'We want to do a deal with you; we want you to be a part of us,'" says Shane the Dribble Machine, shaking his head as though he still can't quite believe it.

The next day, a similar scene plays out in a vastly dissimilar setting. Late at night in And 1's offices, Berger, Gilbert, and a rotating stream of others sit around, reenacting old playground plays and high-fiving. Someone calls NBA star Scottie Pippen a "punk-ass" for seeming to quit on the Houston Rockets. Gilbert even talks a little trash about the industry behemoth: "I dare you to find a swoosh on anybody's arm who doesn't work at Nike." When it is pointed out to Berger that this gathering is not so far removed, in tone or substance, from the one the day before, the one with the better players who have cooler nicknames, he smiles. "That's what this is all about," he says. "Those guys are about the soul of the game and so are we."

12

Even the Ball Is White

IT'S AT MOMENTS like these that Stanley King feels what it's like to be one of his players. Baseball's most prominent African American agent, he paces his Voorhees, New Jersey, office, his adrenaline surging like that of an up-and-coming southpaw with a lead in the bottom of the ninth, facing the heart of the Yankees' order. The pressure is on because on this spring day in 1999, Stanley King has to stare down Scott Boras, who is out to steal his most prized player.

Boras is baseball's most feared and despised agent, the man who incensed the Phillies over phenom J. D. Drew and whom many blame for the off-season's stratospheric rise in salaries. The commissioner's office calls him "an affront to the game."

Boras usually gets what he wants. And now he wants Dernell Stenson, a twenty-year-old outfielder in the Boston Red Sox system who signed with King right out of high school. This morning, Stenson's mom called to tell King that Dernell has been receiving constant phone calls from a young kid named Anthony, who works for Boras. That's not all: Anthony has two round-trip tickets to Los Angeles this weekend – one for him, one for Dernell – where they will have an audience with Boras.

"In this business," King says in a soft, high-pitched voice, "'crisis' is just another word for opportunity." He's trying to psyche himself up.

Baseball America, the bible of minor-league ball, is on King's desk, dog-eared to the pages of hype about Stenson, a power-hitting potential Gold Glove winner who socked twenty-four homers for the Trenton Thunder last season. By all accounts, he is the probable successor to Red Sox superstar first baseman Mo Vaughn, who recently bolted Boston for $80 million in Anaheim.

Stenson is potentially worth that much to King. In pro sports, one player can make an agent's career, and at forty-one, King has found that player in Stenson. "I've got other good players, but he's my entire future," he says. "He's my Secretariat."

When Stenson's mother told King of the calls from Boras's proxy – Anthony – King's first step was to pepper her with questions. As he suspected, Anthony is black. "See, this is the first time Boras has hired a black runner, and that's a direct response to people like me," King says. Seeking to bridge cultural gaps, many established white agents are now hiring black "runners" to recruit for them. "A runner's job is to befriend your player and muddy the water. To start telling your player that you're all about greed, that you should have gotten him a better deal by now. It's like the equivalent of somebody constantly hitting on your wife. She's trying to be a faithful wife, and every day now she's getting all these *Playgirl* magazine models calling her up and hitting on her."

King takes a break from pacing and heads down the hall of his agency, First Round Sports, which he and partner Al Irby started eleven years ago. He checks that a letter is being drafted to Boras, threatening legal action if his runner doesn't cease and desist from harassing Stenson. Then it's back to his office for more pacing. "I've been around enough to know that this kind of thing happens all the time in this business," he says. "But when it's Boras, you have to pay attention. It's a different level of intensity when it's Boras."

As King speaks, hands cutting the air around him, framed portraits of Malcolm X, Martin Luther King Jr., and Muhammad Ali stare down from the walls. "Every decision I make comes from the type of social justice the guys on my wall stood for," he says, looking at the portraits and then down at the phone, which will soon ring with very good – or very, very bad – news.

WITH THE possible exception of the armed services, the field of professional sports in the last two decades has become America's leading meritocracy. If you can hit .300 or score twenty points per game, chances are you'll have an opportunity, no matter the color of your skin. It's only been fifty-four years since Jackie Robinson first integrated pro sports, but there are now fifteen hundred professional black athletes in the United States – 80 percent of the NBA, 67 percent of the NFL, and 17 percent of Major League Baseball. Still, a new generation of agents – who, like King, are black – say that if the profession is color-blind, it's only on the playing field. Just 8 percent of black athletes have black agents.

In basketball, the issue crept into view when rap impresario Puff Daddy is said to have tried to lure 76er guard Allen Iverson away from white *über*-agent David Falk. Another rap entrepreneur, Master P, signed Falk client Ron Mercer, as well as Derek Anderson and football's Heisman Trophy–winning Ricky Williams. Johnnie Cochran, seeing an opportunity, has also registered as an agent. "I have made a career of representing these people – you know, Tupac Shakur," he told HBO's *Real Sports* in 1997. "I think I can relate to younger people."

Considering that Tupac ended up dead, Cochran might want to come up with a more persuasive pitch. But there's no denying the trend: Black businesspeople and attorneys are starting to lay claim to black athletes, and white agents are crying foul.

The first loud whistle was blown five years ago, when NBA all-star guard Penny Hardaway of the Orlando Magic hired black agents Carl and Kevin Poston. Immediately, Hardaway heard from detractors who told him that the Postons were playing the race card – and playing him for a fool.

"But Penny withstood that pressure," Stan King observes, once again nervously leafing through the *Baseball America* on his desk. "And that's what I have to do with Dernell. Help him be strong enough to withstand the pressure from Boras and others."

Unlike basketball, baseball is still a white player's game. King recruits only black players and, to a lesser degree, Latinos. "That's because of what I call the 'comfort level hurdle,'" he says, smiling at the seemingly simplistic phrase that, he knows, conjures all sorts of race-related issues. "White players are more comfortable hiring white agents, and it's just not a good use of my time to go after whites. Of course, that doesn't stop white agents from going after black players." Stenson, for instance, receives twenty to thirty voice-mail messages a day from white agents seeking his business.

King represents some twenty-five minor leaguers and a handful of majors. He repped three Phillies on the 1993 World Series Team: Milt Thompson, Tony Longmire, and Ben Rivera. This 1999–2000 season could be his breakout year, as a handful of King clients are vying for big-league spots. In Minnesota, Brian Richardson and Christian Guzman are competing for the starting third baseman and shortstop slots, respectively. Here in Philly, King's got Tyrone Horne, a left-handed outfielder who smacked thirty-seven homers in Double A ball in 1998 en route to Texas League player-of-the-year honors. And of course, there's Stenson in Boston.

In all these cases, King didn't recruit by using race explicitly; he didn't have to. He simply tries to sell a kid on the kid's own "comfort level."

"These kids today look at the money Boras is getting guys, and they really think it's about what the agent did," King says. "I tell them, no player gets $100 million because of his agent. It doesn't work that way. They really think it's not their talent – it's you. I try to tell them they should focus on hiring someone who is competent but who, above all else, they're comfortable with."

Established agents argue, however, that, by preaching about "comfort level," King is subtly playing the race card, using a sophisticated euphemism to manipulate kids into signing with him because they share his skin color. "I can't help that I'm white and Jewish," says Penn Valley native Arn Tellem, who represents the Orioles' Albert Belle, the Phils' Doug Glanville, and L.A. Laker Kobe Bryant. "What I tell players is that I offer them expertise, and it shouldn't be about anything else. But this is a very competitive business, and a lot of times black agents will make an issue out of race because it's to their advantage."

Then again, King claims he's up against something Boras and Tellem will never have to confront: Call it "blacklash," a widespread perception among black athletes – and their families – that black agents just don't measure up, especially compared with white, Jewish lawyers. Kevin Poston, Hardaway's agent, tells the story of the kid who, on hearing that Poston had a swimming pool in his backyard, asked if he dealt drugs. King recalls a mother who chose a white, Jewish agent over him because "it says in the Bible they're the chosen people, and everything they touch, they make money at."

"At least she was honest," King says. We've left the silence of his office phone for the Cap'n Cat Clam Bar, an unassuming spot in Voorhees where King delights in taking millionaire jocks. "More often, you sense there's something subtle going on that they don't want to talk about."

Still, once in a while, a client will come along who sees hiring King as a means of racial empowerment. Such was the case with Ray Lankford, the center fielder of the St. Louis Cardinals, whose previous contract negotiation, for $13 million over three years, had been handled by big-time white agent Jeff Moorad – partner of the well-known Leigh Steinberg. King had worked on some side business deals for Lankford, who sensed something different in King. "I began to realize that what I grew up believing wasn't necessarily true," Lankford says. "See, as a kid, you always got that sense that to be successful, you needed a white guy to guide you. And then I met Stan, who, unlike any other agent I spoke to, made it clear he worked for me, not the other way around, and who preached to me about thinking about life after sports. And since we're both black, we had a lot in common."

Lankford asked King to do his latest deal for him, a five-year, $35 million contract that is the largest ever in baseball for a black agent. Today, King likes to say he sold Lankford on his services by borrowing a line from Jerry Maguire: "Help me help you."

"The magic isn't me, it's in you, Ray," King told him. "You're the straw that stirs the drink. I've spent my whole life making arguments, and I can sell people on you if you put up the numbers."

But Lankford was as attracted by King's sociopolitical preachings as his bottom-line reasoning. Lankford, who oversees a charitable foundation in inner-city St. Louis, saw that King had a similar commitment to "give back." King organized an annual Negro League Award Ceremony, has been active in a charitable group called Concerned Black Men of Philadelphia, and has been a mentor to would-be inner-city businesspeople as a part of the Philadelphia Youth Entrepreneurial Institute. Lankford saw that Delino DeShields — then a King client — wore his socks high during the summer that celebrated Jackie Robinson's breaking of the color line, a style tribute to Negro League players. And he listened to King lambaste black athletes who were solely interested in inking the next deal.

"The African American community has one of the greatest resources going," King often preaches. "Sports is the fastest growing industry in America, probably bigger than steel in the twenties. I'm saying that if Michael Jordan wanted to, he could stand up and tell Nike to make sneakers in Camden or Bed-Stuy rather than Korea. But it's a lack of vision and commitment. He has the power. In baseball, guys like Bonds and Griffey have the power. But they won't use it."

"A lot of guys today are narrow-minded," agrees Lankford. "They need to look in the mirror."

Lankford — no Bonds or Griffey in terms of on- or off-field clout — is the exception. Dernell Stenson, however, could be the next Bonds or Griffey.

BACK IN HIS OFFICE after lunch, King isn't even pretending to do other work. He's at his desk, idly chatting, waiting for a call from a twenty-year-old ballplayer that could cost him millions.

Calls like these are commonplace in the agent business. Every agent has a story about the one who got away, the kid on whom he spent hours and thousands only to have the phone ring late one night and hear, "Thanks for all the good times, but I'm going with someone else."

"I've had Dernell for three years and haven't taken a dime," King says, leaning forward. "I've spent thousands – on plane tickets, meals, the best equipment. Because he's an investment. But it's not just about the money. It's about the whole package."

All along, Stenson has represented the melding of King's professional and sociopolitical visions. Stenson can make him rich, powerful, and able to enact social change within baseball. The last thing King wants is to become just another agent, doing deals for the quick score.

Two bookcases in King's office announce his passions. The shelves are filled with biographies of Ali and Robinson and tomes such as Nelson George's *Elevating the Game: The History and Aesthetics of Black Men and Basketball*. He discusses the books animatedly, but he never forgets the nearby phone, noticeable for its deafening silence. As King talks about his role models, and as they look on from his walls, it becomes clear: Stenson just might be the key to keeping King's lifelong idealism alive.

Before moving to Brooklyn at age eleven, Stan King lived in a fifth-floor Bronx walk-up, right next to the infamous Fort Apache police precinct. The sounds of suspects being beaten inside the precinct house serenaded King through the thin tenement walls every day.

King experienced his first political moments in that cramped apartment. It was from there that his older brother and role model, Norris, left to serve in Japan during the Vietnam War; he'd return home sporting an Afro and reading Eldridge Cleaver's *Soul on Ice*. Their immigrant parents, who had come from the Virgin Islands to make a life in New York, didn't understand concepts such as "Black Power."

It was in that living room, with the sounds of police brutality constantly in the air, that King watched the 1968 Olympics. "I can still see it today," he says slowly, closing his eyes. "How John Carlos and Tommy Smith first bowed their heads, took their shoes off, and raised their black leather gloves in a clenched fist during the National Anthem. I was ten, but I sat there a long time, all choked up. Because I knew they were taking a stand for me and people who looked like me, even for the people being beaten on the other side of the wall."

In the late sixties and early seventies, the Zeitgeist in sports reflected the times at large. It was a generation before the megabucks of endorsement money would stop black athletes from speaking out. And King soaked it all in – how his heroes Martin Luther King Jr. and Malcolm X had set the agenda, and how Ali followed by opposing the war. But not just Ali; what resonated for King was the procession of black athletes who supported Ali's stand, including (then) Lew Alcindor, Rafer Johnson, and Jim Brown.

But all that is history. Today, our sports rarely reflect the political, as they did during Stan King's youth. King's circumstances, if not his ideology, have come a long way since then, too. He lives in Washington Township, New Jersey, with his wife, Sharon; their two-year-old child, Norris; Stan's two kids from his first marriage; and Sharon's two kids.

King graduated from Oglethorpe University in three years and, later, from Rutgers Law School, where he decided to meld his passion for social justice with his love of sports.

When his childhood friend, baseball star Willie Randolph, introduced him to the Dodgers' Mike Sharperson, who happened to be looking for an agent, the fledgling First Round Sports had its first big name. Other players began to notice King; Sharperson, who died in 1997 in a car accident, spread the word about him. Cardinals' shortstop Ozzie Smith, who never used an agent for contract negotiations, began to solicit advice from King and spoke well of him in the clubhouse. Gradually, as his stable came to include Lankford and Delino DeShields, King became a player in Major League Baseball backrooms. Today, he frequently addresses the American Bar Association and countless law schools on the business of sports.

Harder to effect has been King's dream of empowering his clients with some sense of social consciousness. "I realized that if I'm going to be William Kunstler, I'm going to starve out here," he says. His modus operandi has turned more subtle. "I heard [University of Louisville coach] Denny Crum once say, 'Give me any kid who can run and jump, and I'll teach him to play basketball.' Well, give me any kid who likes me, who is a good athlete and trusts me with his business, and I'll turn him into a Ray Lankford over time, just by being an example. Because I know my cause is right. I know I'm articulating a position that's morally right, and that will rub off."

But getting the chance to do it has been the hard part. King defers to nobody when criticizing baseball's record on race—he calls RBI, the sport's Reviving Baseball in the Inner-cities program, an underfunded "joke"—but he reserves his sharpest barbs for black players who decry the sport's racism while doing nothing to counter it. "You know, these guys can point the finger at Major League Baseball,

saying, 'We want more black managers and front-office people,' but they don't answer when you ask, 'Who is your agent?
Who is your accountant?' 'Cause they know, if they're not
hiring me, they're not being represented by an African American. So they choose not to. Don't get me wrong. They love
me to death. They'll give me anything I ask for, other than
their business."

This is Stan King's life today. He lives in Jersey but devotes
time and money to Philly causes. He is a fixture at the jazz
club Zanzibar Blue. And he attends baseball's agent meetings, where he is often the lone black face in the room and
finds himself one of the sport's few voices pushing for sensitivity. Yet when he tries to recruit black athletes, he can't help
but feel he's the recipient of black-on-black prejudice. It's a
vexing dichotomy. "My biggest challenge is not to get discouraged," he admits.

Whatever slights he may receive from his own kind, his
inner Kunstler can't help but find its voice. In the summer of
1998, when Mark McGwire and Sammy Sosa riveted the nation, King recognized the underlying racial narrative. "I affectionately call Sammy 'Uncle Sammy,' just in a joking way,
because he had to be ingratiating," King says. "If he looked
like he was embittered by the home-run race and wanted to
kick Mark's ass, then this whole society would have turned
on him. It would have been seen as him taking something
from 'us,' right? Like, 'Who the hell does this Dominican
think he is?' So instead Sammy says, 'You're the man in
America, I'm the man in the Dominican. I love Mark Mc-
Gwire.' And it worked. He now has a McDonald's deal."

Similarly, when baseball insiders seem mystified that the
sport is still accused of racism, King doesn't pull punches. "I
don't think white people in baseball are sitting around say-

ing, 'How can we fuck black people today?'" he says. "But you can't deny race in the equation. Look at Kevin Stocker. Not taking anything away from Kev, but if you're black and you hit .220, you don't make the bigs. When the Phillies had an all-white roster a couple of years ago, I'm sure it wasn't by design. But the marginal player – the guy they wanted to give a break – the benefit went to the white one. That's how it works, and it's not going to change until the balance of power shifts."

He's in full Kunstler mode now but interrupts himself to check his watch. Though all this highfalutin theorizing is fun, it won't pay the bills, and it damn sure won't put the kids through college.

At 4 P.M., Dernell Stenson's call is put through. "This should be interesting," King mutters as he gets himself set, like a batter going through his rituals in the box. He picks up the receiver and, leaning back, cradles it against his shoulder. Only when he's finally ready does he reach forward and press the button on the phone that gives him the voice of his future.

"Hey, Dern!" King's voice is loud and friendly as he starts talking and talking and talking, as if the bad news can be avoided through the sheer drumbeat of his voice. He begins by telling Stenson that he spoke with the big-league club, and they're excited he's heading down early to spring training, and they'll even give him 24 cents per mile a day while he's in Ft. Myers, Florida. And here's the kicker: They'll pay for his meals and put him up at the Sheraton – a big-league hotel. "It'll be good to get out of those Days Inns, huh Dern?" he says, laughing.

On the other end of the phone, Stenson is pumped to be so wanted in a big-league camp, and that's just as King would have it. Now he can get to the point. "So, Dern, tell me about this Anthony kid, Scott Boras's guy," he says, half-smile frozen in place.

"Aw, Stan, that kid's just doing his job," Stenson says.

There's a pause.

"Uh-huh," King says.

"Don't worry, Stan," Stenson says.

"Okay," King says. Now comes the key question, King knows: "What about going to Los Angeles with him this weekend?"

"Hell, I ain't going to L.A., man," Stenson says.

King finally allows himself a smile. "'Cause you know what this kid is all about, Dern. Scott's hiring this kid to get him players, especially black players. How much you want to bet this Anthony kid ain't talking to Scott Rolen?" he asks, referring to the Phils' third baseman, one of the sport's "great white hopes."

They both laugh, and then King is closing the conversation, inviting Stenson to accompany him and Lankford to the Super Bowl. Stenson says goodbye, and King's face widens into an ear-to-ear grin.

"Oh, man, that's a big one right there," he says. "Oh, man."

Smiling, sighing, Stan King hangs up the phone with his right hand. His left hand, fist clenched, raises in victory— even though nothing, in the final analysis, has really happened. The day ends as it began, with Stenson holding the key to King's career; and yet Stan King heads home, victorious.

13

Jelly Maker

MUHAMMAD ALI has been hot ever since, with shaky hand and placid expression, he lit the torch to open the 1996 Olympics. There has been an Academy Award–winning documentary, a best-selling book, countless magazine covers – even the front of a Wheaties box, an honor never before bestowed on the fighter once known as "The Louisville Lip." But when Ali had the power of speech, his public image was decidedly different. Draft resister and black nationalist, Ali was a threat to white America in the late sixties, long before the rap group Public Enemy coined the phrase "Fear of a Black Planet."

Now, some thirty years later, a softer, cuddlier Ali is celebrated. Silenced by Parkinson's disease (a degenerative nerve condition), he is consistently praised for his commitment to principle, and he is served up as an antidote for today's greedy, self-centered professional athlete. Time and again the myopic press tells us that this generation's icons would do well to follow Ali's socially conscious lead.

When Michael Jordan announced his retirement from basketball in 1999, the comparisons to Ali began flying fast and furious. In terms of social impact, the conventional wisdom went, Jordan comes up short. It started at his farewell press conference, when Jordan was asked if he might now try to help "solve some of the world's problems."

"I can't solve the world's problems," Jordan responded, noting that he still had TV commercials to star in, golf to play, and kids to raise. The *New York Times'* Ira Berkow wouldn't take no for an answer. "If he isn't playing basketball, he should have enough time to read up on issues," he wrote.

"Jordan uses his clout to peddle sneakers and star in unwatchable movies with Bugs Bunny, leaving the very distinct impression that he has the social consciousness of a baked potato," agreed John Schulian in the pages of *GQ,* in a piece that named Ali the athlete of the century.

And now comes *Redemption Song: Muhammad Ali and the Spirit of Sixties,* a compelling reminder of just how revolutionary Ali was. But even Michael Marqusee can't refrain from dissing Jordan in light of Ali, arguing that Jordan's "blackness has been deliberately submerged within his Americanness, which is reduced, in the end, to his individual wealth and success."

More than thirty years ago, Ali scoffed at the patronizing press that had dubbed Joe Louis "a credit to his race" and found Ali threatening. "I don't have to be what you want me to be," he said then. Ironically, Jordan, famous for the marketing tag line "Be Like Mike," has been criticized by the likes of Jesse Jackson, Arthur Ashe, Jim Brown, and a white liberal press for not being like Ali.

Just as the conventional wisdom about Ali was off-base three decades ago, so, too, is this reevaluation of Jordan, this notion that he stands for nothing more lofty than enriching his own bank account. Maybe history will repeat itself and, in thirty years, the American media will do another about-face and begin to credit Jordan as a truly groundbreaking figure.

The anti-Jordan camp has gained momentum recently. There was his silence over Nike's use of cheap overseas labor. Then he refused to endorse Harvey Gantt, a credible black challenger to Senator Jesse Helms in Jordan's home state of North Carolina. "Our situation is increasingly desperate, and I admire those athletes and entertainers who consciously try to give something back to people," wrote Ashe in his posthumously published autobiography, *Days of Grace.* "I am less happy with the demureness of someone like Michael Jordan, who is as popular as he is rich. While I defend Jordan's right to stay out of politics in general, I think he made a mistake in declining to give any open support to Harvey Gantt."

But while Jordan came in for criticism, no one was peppering tennis star Pete Sampras, another Nike endorser, with political questions. Nor were any pundits demanding that Bill Gates endorse candidates for public office. Was it Jordan's skin color that singled him out for spokesman status?

The assumption that Jordan would support Gantt because both are black told more about how the pundits viewed African Americans – as a monolithic voting bloc – than it did about Jordan.

The demand that Jordan be an Ali-like spokesman for his people grows out of a civil rights–era mindset, and Jordan is part of a post–civil rights generation, the first to attain a modicum of power from within the establishment. In this cultural moment, Jordan doesn't matter so much for what he says as for what he's done. He has undermined countless stereotypes, the very caricatures that underpin the racism decried by his liberal critics. After all, he is not lazy, unintel-

ligent, inarticulate, or, most important, incapable of handling money.

"Ali's politics grew out of the times," says Todd Boyd, professor of critical studies at the University of Southern California and author of the 1997 book *Am I Black Enough for
You?* "But Jordan's presence assumes a political stance. The
fact that he exists has political significance."

Jesse Jackson is fond of saying, "There are tree shakers,
and there are jelly makers." Until Jordan, however, black
athletes opted exclusively for the shake. From Ali to Tommy
Smith and John Carlos at the 1968 Olympics to Charles
Barkley's pledge to be a "nineties nigga – we do what we
want to," the socially conscious black athlete's role was to
rail publicly against injustice. But then along came Jordan,
who was more interested in making the jelly, in accumulat-
ing power by parlaying his athletic talent into a business
empire now valued at some $500 million. Today, his true
legacy lies in a new generation of black jocks who see that
they can leverage their sports careers into economic empowerment.

"I wouldn't have started these businesses if I hadn't
watched Michael these last few years," says Chris Webber,
star forward for the Sacramento Kings and owner of a Gold's
Gym franchise and a recording label that employs black people in his hometown of Detroit. "He's showed me that I could
be more than just an athlete." Webber is not an aberration.
Athletes evolving into business entities, seeing themselves
as entrepreneurs, has become the norm now. Basketball star
Grant Hill has dumped his management company and taken
his career into his own hands. "Michael's led the way for
what I'm doing now," he says. Similarly, basketball's Allen
Iverson fired Jordan's longtime agent David Falk and now

has plans for his own line of hip-hop clothing. Football star Keyshawn Johnson – in the NFL for all of three years – in 1999 opened Reign, a trendy Los Angeles restaurant. And do you believe for a moment that, before each and every business decision, Tiger Woods doesn't ask himself, "What would Mike do?"

For all his visibility, Ali never had such impact. In fact, Ali went broke, as did Joe Louis and Kareem Abdul-Jabbar. Single-handedly, Jordan made himself into a refutation of the "nigger-rich" stereotype long fostered by the business failings of other athletes.

Ali had media cachet but lacked the power even to stand up to Don King, the scourge of his own sport. Yes, Ali's rhetoric was enchanting, but he was never able to flex his muscles as Jordan did recently when he walked away from buying into the Charlotte Hornets because he wasn't being given enough control (thereby forever sealing the reputation of that team's owner as the guy who stood in the way of the hometown savior rescuing the franchise).

Just as Ali's outspokenness was of his time, so too are Jordan's boardroom moves. Jordan came of age along with hip-hop (even though his musical tastes run more to the likes of Luther Vandross), in which artist-entrepreneurs such as Chuck D, Puff Daddy, and Master P have focused on controlling the means of production in addition to being the product. Ironically, Ali's defiance, not to mention his legendary rhymes, informs their art. But Jordan's business acumen has had an equally important, practical impact; from Jordan they got the message that, in the words of USC's Boyd, they could "empower themselves by capitalizing on their image – and that any sense of self-determination that comes from that is truly political, because it's liberating."

And speaking of hip-hop, it bears noting that the demand for Jordan to become overtly political might just make a prophet out of rapper Ice-T, who released an album a decade ago subtitled *Freedom of Speech . . . Just Watch What You Say.* Jordan may have sensed the disingenuousness of those who called on him to speak out; would they be so eager to hear views that didn't follow the party line? In fact, though it may disappoint Berkow and his ilk, there is scant evidence that Jordan is passionate about speaking on behalf of the disenfranchised. There is, however, ample proof that he gets worked up arguing for free-market principles, as he did during 1999's NBA lockout. In that dispute, he lambasted the league's owners, all of whom had made fortunes as capitalists but wanted their laborers to accept an artificial cap on their salaries. To the media, Jordan suddenly personified the greed of today's athlete. One can't help wondering if that was because, in taking a public stand normally articulated by white men of his tax bracket, he'd violated the media-approved, Ali-informed "black athlete as spokesman for the underclass" script.

Besides, if the press were truly interested in an athlete breaking new political ground, Jordan's flamboyant former teammate, Dennis Rodman, would have been lauded by the macho sports press instead of jeered when he spoke in favor of gay rights. (Or dismissed as a publicity hound when he paid for the funeral of James Byrd, the black man in Texas who was tied to a pickup truck and dragged to his death by white supremacists.)

Jordan has often said that he doesn't know enough about politics to wade into it, and it makes perfect sense that someone who so diligently prepared for basketball games would want to be just as well versed before engaging in another type of public battle. After all, our athletes are among the least equipped among us to hold their own in matters of state, for they are prodigies: They've been raised to work and focus on one thing to the exclusion of almost all else. Self-absorption is practically part of the job description.

Yet the demand for athletes to somehow morally lead us continues. When the bait is taken, the whole dynamic has the stench of a media setup – something Jordan smelled back in 1992, when, in a *Playboy* interview, he responded to his liberal critics by saying, "Don't knock me off that pedestal that you wanted me to get on to."

Others haven't been quite as perceptive. Witness the rambling, bigoted comments of recently retired NFL star and ordained minister Reggie White, who told the Wisconsin legislature that Puerto Ricans have a skill for "fitting forty people in an apartment" and American Indians "knew how to sneak up on people." Listening to White, one couldn't help wondering: What genius provided the forum for this?

Those who invoke the legacy of Ali to goad the likes of White or Jordan into answering big-picture questions never posed to Sampras or Cal Ripken seem to have conveniently forgotten that circumstances helped turn Ali into a sociopolitical icon. Had he not been drafted into the military, he would have simply been another great boxer. Jordan has been confronted with no such reason to be anything more than what he is – a true symbol of the American Dream, owner of a narrative that begins with talent and hard work and ends in stunning wealth and personal empowerment.

Besides, there is evidence that Jordan would regret heeding the call to enter the political fray. Jackie Robinson did get involved in politics toward the end of his life, and he emerged bitter for the experience. As he wrote in his 1972 autobiography, in the 1940s "I had more faith in the ultimate justice of the American white man than I have today." What Robinson came to realize, too late, was that by breaking baseball's color line, he didn't need to say anything. He made one of the century's most eloquent political statements every time he walked out on the field.

Here's hoping that Michael Jordan will learn from Robinson's dying regret – and that, rather than being in conflict, the roles of Ali and Jordan will come to be seen as part of a continuum: Ali as tree shaker, helping to make a jelly maker like Jordan possible.

Acknowledgments

FIRST, I AM indebted to Micah Kleit and his colleagues at Temple University Press. This book would have never come to fruition were it not for Micah's vision and encouraging words.

For over a decade, I've conned a host of editors into paying me for writing, and without fail they have all saved me from my worst instincts: Eliot Kaplan, Ilena Silverman, Stephen Fried, Bill Shapiro, Laura Miller, Doug Cruikshank, Mark Cohen, Mark Adams, Zack Stalberg, Michael Hainey, Jon Gluck, Duane Swierczynski, Marty Beiser, Tim Whitaker, and, especially, Loren Feldman, a good friend. In addition, Herb and David Lipson of *Philadelphia Magazine* have provided me with a comfortable, if sometimes comically dysfunctional, home.

As always, David Black is a great friend and an even better agent.

There have also been a host of colleagues and friends over the years on whose wisdom I often relied while penning these pieces. That list includes a Dream Team of guys you want to watch big games with: Scott MacDonald, Andrew Corsello, my roomie Bob Huber, Joey Joe Martell, Ken Shropshire, and Bob Baber, who is not only a great friend and frequent hardcourt foil, but who also proofread and edited these pieces prior to publication. In addition, a special thanks to Ben Gay Wallace, whose journey of sexual self-discovery has been edifying for all who know him. And I take comfort in the knowledge that, no matter where I am, if Iain Levison is there as well, I'm not the most immature person in the room.

Editorial assistant Kevin McGuire transcribed tape and typed up more of the Platt canon than any one human being ought to be subjected to. He not only worked tirelessly but always did so in good cheer. A special thanks to my mother, Sondra Platt, whose one rule during my adolescence was that any request for a book was to be granted immediately. And to my sister Bethann, the only travel agent I know willing to supply the safety records of major airlines.

I am indebted to all of those who have let me write about them, particularly my own personal gallery of quirky role models: Tex Cobb, Janet Ake, Eric Riley, John Lucas, Vernon Maxwell, Pat Croce, and Charles Barkley.

Finally, I'm not there yet, but I'm still working on being worthy of Bet, who every day shows me what it means to be human, caring, and kind. I'm very lucky. (How sweet is that?)